Conspiracy Theories

T0087549

Introducing Polity's new series:
little books that make you THINK.

Quassim Cassam, *Conspiracy Theories*
Stephen Mumford, *Football*
Shannon Sullivan, *White Privilege*

Quassim Cassam

Conspiracy Theories

polity

The right of Quassim Cassam to be identified as Author of this Work has been asserted in accordance with the UK Copyright, Designs and Patents Act 1988.

First published in 2019 by Polity Press

Reprinted 2019 (twice), 2020 (five times), 2021

Polity Press
65 Bridge Street
Cambridge CB2 1UR, UK

Polity Press
101 Station Landing
Suite 300
Medford, MA 02155, USA

ISBN-13: 978-1-5095-3582-8
ISBN-13: 978-1-5095-3583-5(pb)

A catalogue record for this book is available from the British Library.

Library of Congress Cataloging-in-Publication Data
Names: Cassam, Quassim, author.
Title: Conspiracy theories / Quassim Cassam.
Description: Cambridge, UK ; Medford, MA : Polity Press, [2019] | Series:
  Think
Identifiers: LCCN 2019008492 (print) | LCCN 2019010406 (ebook) | ISBN
  9781509535842 (Epub) | ISBN 9781509535828 (hardback) | ISBN
9781509535835
  (pbk.)
Subjects: LCSH: Conspiracy theories.
Classification: LCC HV6275 (ebook) | LCC HV6275 .C36 2019 (print) | DDC
  001.9--dc23
LC record available at https://lccn.loc.gov/2019008492

Typeset in 11 on 15 Sabon
by Fakenham Prepress Solutions, Fakenham, Norfolk, NR21 8NL
Printed and bound in the United States by LSC Communications

The publisher has used its best endeavours to ensure that the URLs for external websites referred to in this book are correct and active at the time of going to press. However, the publisher has no responsibility for the websites and can make no guarantee that a site will remain live or that the content is or will remain appropriate.

Every effort has been made to trace all copyright holders, but if any have been overlooked the publisher will be pleased to include any necessary credits in any subsequent reprint or edition.

For further information on Polity, visit our website: politybooks.com

Contents

Preface

Back in 2015, in an article for the digital magazine *Aeon*, I discussed the intellectual character of conspiracy theorists. I was influenced by Susan Stebbing's famous observation that there is an urgent need today for the citizens of a democracy to think well. My idea in the *Aeon* article was that conspiracy theories were often the result of bad thinking and of the intellectual character traits that result in bad thinking.

Since the publication of my *Aeon* article, my take on conspiracy theories has changed. I have come around to the view that they need to be understood first and foremost in political terms, and that the intellectual character of conspiracy theorists is a side issue. For example, even if there is something wrong with the thinking behind conspiracy theories about the Holocaust, that is hardly the main issue with such theories and the people who promote them. The fundamental issues here are political and, indeed, ethical.

This book is about the politics of conspiracy theories. My claim is that they are basically a form of political propaganda and that the response to them also needs to be political. Although I'm a philosopher, it seems to me that many philosophers who write about conspiracy theories miss their real point. I have tried to put that right here.

I know from previous experience that criticising conspiracy theories and conspiracy theorists is a tricky business. The reaction to my *Aeon* article was explosive and I don't suppose that what I say in this book will be any more palatable to conspiracy theorists and their apologists. I hope I am better prepared this time. To write about conspiracy theories you need a thick skin, unless you are actually promoting a conspiracy theory.

I thank Pascal Porcheron for persuading to me write this book and for very helpful comments on earlier drafts. I also thank Naomi Eilan and Deborah Ghate for many other helpful comments and discussions.

1

The (Real) Point of Conspiracy Theories

Conspiracy theorists get a seriously bad press. Gullible, irresponsible, paranoid, stupid. These are some of the politer labels applied to them, usually by establishment figures who aren't averse to promoting their own conspiracy theories when it suits them. President George W. Bush denounced outrageous conspiracy theories about 9/11 while his own administration was busy promoting the outrageous conspiracy theory that Iraq was behind 9/11, in cahoots with Al Qaeda.

If the abuse isn't bad enough, conspiracy theorists now have the dubious privilege of being studied by psychologists. The psychology of conspiracy theories is a thing, and the news for conspiracy theorists isn't good. A recent study describes their theories as corrosive to societal and individual well-being.[1] Conspiracy theorists, the study reveals, are more likely to be male, unmarried, and less educated, to have lower household incomes, and to see themselves as being of low social standing. They have lower levels of physical and psychological well-being and are more likely to meet the criteria for having a psychiatric disorder.

In case you're starting to feel sorry for conspiracy theorists (or for yourself, if you are one), perhaps it's worth remembering that they aren't exactly shrinking violets. They are vociferous defenders of their theories and scornful of their opponents. Anyone who has been on the receiving end of the wrath of conspiracy theorists will know that it can be a bruising experience. I have the honour of being described by one eminent (if that's the right word) conspiracy theorist and fellow philosopher as a 'bona fide anti-conspiracy buffoon'.[2]

And yet, on reflection, you might wonder what all the fuss is about. After all, if a conspiracy theorist is someone who believes in the existence

---

[1] D. Freeman and R. Bentall, 'The concomitants of conspiracy concerns', *Social Psychiatry and Psychiatric Epidemiology* 52 (2017): 595–604.

[2] The name of my admirer is James Fetzer. There is more on him below.

of some conspiracies, then surely in that sense we are *all* conspiracy theorists. History is full of well-documented conspiracies and one would have to be remarkably ignorant not to realise that. Michael Moore once said that he wasn't into conspiracy theories 'except the ones that are true'.[3] Realistically, isn't that actually the position we're all in? Surely what we should be debating is not whether there is anything wrong with conspiracy theories per se, but whether there is anything wrong with specific conspiracy theories.

According to the 9/11 conspiracy theorist James Fetzer (that's the guy who thinks I'm an anti-conspiracy buffoon), for something to qualify as a 'conspiracy', it only requires two or more people who collaborate to perpetrate an illegal act. There are a couple of important things missing from this definition: conspiracies are supposed to be *secret* and, because of that, they involve a *small* group of people – the conspirators. A conspiracy requires a small group of conspirators who work together in secret to do something illegal or harmful.

This is the sense of 'conspiracy' according to which history has always been full of conspiracies.

---

[3] Or involve dentists. See Michael Moore, *Dude, Where's My Country?* (Warner Books, 2003), p. 2.

The (Real) Point of Conspiracy Theories

Suppose that a conspiracy *theory* is defined as a theory about a conspiracy. In that case, history books are full of conspiracy theories. They tell us, for example, that Guy Fawkes and his colleagues plotted to blow up the English parliament in 1605. The plot was a conspiracy by Fetzer's definition and mine, and historical accounts of the plot are therefore conspiracy theories.

You don't have to go back to 1605 for examples of conspiracy theories. There are lots of conspiracy theories about 9/11, the attacks on New York and Washington on 11 September 2001 – and I don't just mean theories to the effect that the Bush administration or Iraq was behind them. By the definition of 'conspiracy theory' I've just given, the official account of 9/11, as set out in the official report of the 9/11 Commission, is also a conspiracy theory. That account says that the 9/11 attacks were carried out by nineteen Al Qaeda operatives who collaborated in secret to do something immensely harmful to the United States government and to thousands of its citizens. That's a conspiracy in anyone's money.

So it seems that, if you believe the official account of 9/11, then you're a conspiracy theorist. And if you don't believe the official account, you're still a conspiracy theorist. Either way you're a conspiracy

4

theorist; and pretty much everyone else is one too. In that case, how can there be a debate about whether one should be a conspiracy theorist, that is, believe that conspiracies happen?

What's more, if many conspiracy theories are true, then how can it possibly be corrosive to societal and individual well-being to be a conspiracy theorist, to believe that some conspiracy theories are true? If we are *all* conspiracy theorists, then it doesn't make sense to say that conspiracy theorists are less educated (than whom?) or more likely to meet the criteria for having a psychiatric disorder. That would be absurd, and the 'psychology of conspiracy theories' is starting to look like a total waste of time.

But here's the thing: when people argue about conspiracy theories, they aren't arguing about whether individuals have ever collaborated in secret to perpetrate illegal acts. The conspiracy theories that people actually argue about are different from ordinary tales of conspiracy. In the ordinary sense of 'conspiracy theory', the official account of 9/11 isn't a conspiracy theory. The theory that 9/11 was an inside job is. The theory that in 1605 Guy Fawkes and others conspired to blow up the English parliament in the Gunpowder Plot isn't a conspiracy theory. The theory that the Holocaust is a myth concocted to serve Jewish interests is.

So what's the difference? As it happens, there is a sound rationale for being selective in applying the label 'conspiracy theory'. As conspiracy theory expert Rob Brotherton points out, 'when people call something a conspiracy theory, they're usually not talking about just any old conspiracy'.[4] Conspiracy theories in the ordinary sense are extraordinary. They have a bunch of special features that make them different from accounts of conspiracies like the Gunpowder Plot.

To avoid confusion, I'll call these extraordinary theories 'Conspiracy Theories' with a capital C and a capital T. A Conspiracy Theory isn't just a theory about a conspiracy. There is more to it than that. A Conspiracy Theorist, again with a capital C and a capital T, is a person who is 'into' Conspiracy Theories, that is, unusually fascinated by them and more willing than most to believe them. We are all conspiracy theorists – we all believe that people sometimes get together in secret to do bad things – but we aren't all Conspiracy Theorists.

I don't have a problem with conspiracy theories but I do have a problem with many Conspiracy Theories. Here's one problem: given the features

<hr>

[4] Rob Brotherton, *Suspicious Minds: Why We Believe Conspiracy Theories* (Bloomsbury Sigma, 2015), p. 62.

that make them special, they're unlikely to be true. Conspiracy Theories are implausible by design. Sometimes implausible theories turn out to be true, but it isn't usually sensible to *believe* that they are true. So it isn't usually sensible to be a Conspiracy Theorist. It's no defence to point out that history books are full of tales of conspiracy because, for the most part, these tales aren't Conspiracy Theories in the special sense that I'm talking about.

If Conspiracy Theories are unlikely to be true and some of them – such as the theory that the Holocaust is a myth – have been conclusively refuted, then what's their point? What purpose do Conspiracy Theories serve, if not to tell the truth? And why do people continue to peddle Conspiracy Theories that have virtually no chance of being true? *Because Conspiracy Theories are first and foremost forms of political propaganda.* They are political gambits whose real function is to promote a political agenda. They aren't 'just theories' like any other.

Which political agenda? Sometimes it's not that obvious, but there are lots of examples of Conspiracy Theories whose political agenda you don't have to be a genius to work out. For example, the point of Conspiracy Theories about the Holocaust is to advance the cause of right-wing anti-Semitism.

The (Real) Point of Conspiracy Theories

What these theories are about is exonerating the Nazis and portraying 'the Jews' in as negative a light as possible.

Here's another example, from recent history. Back in 2012 Adam Lanza murdered twenty students and six members of staff at Sandy Hook Elementary School in Newtown, Connecticut. It wasn't long before Conspiracy Theorists started to claim that the whole episode was an elaborate hoax by the government, a classic false flag operation in which no one died. Why would the government want to do such a thing? To push the case for gun control.

If that sounds like a reasonable thing to believe, then the following is no less reasonable: Lanza really did shoot twenty-six people at Sandy Hook, and that was a potential problem for the gun lobby. What better way to pre-empt calls for tighter gun control in the wake of a mass shooting at an elementary school than to claim that the shooting never happened? Take the original Conspiracy Theory, reverse-engineer it, and now it all makes sense: the Sandy Hook conspiracy theory is a blatant piece of political propaganda designed to divert attention from the real problem: the absence of effective gun control in the United States.

This sounds like a conspiracy theory (or should that be Conspiracy Theory?) about Conspiracy

The (Real) Point of Conspiracy Theories

Theories: Conspiracy Theories are part of a conspiracy to advance right-wing political causes. But if my theory is a conspiracy theory, then Conspiracy Theorists shouldn't have a problem with it. There are conspiracy theories about just about everything, so why not conspiracy theories about conspiracy theories and the people who advertise them?

The truth is even more complicated. Saying that Conspiracy Theories about Sandy Hook and other such events are pieces of political propaganda makes it sound as though the peddling of such theories is a conscious and deliberate strategy designed to advance a political cause, the implication being that Sandy Hook Conspiracy Theorists are deliberately spreading what they know to be falsehoods in order to manipulate public opinion.

Even if that implication is true, it's still not a Conspiracy Theory unless the people who manipulate public opinion by spreading falsehoods are working together. I haven't said anything about that. For all I've said, the spreading of Conspiracy Theories could be the work of individual conspiracy entrepreneurs who happen to have the same political objective. If these conspiracy entrepreneurs aren't collaborating, then by definition there is no conspiracy. But there's also a subtler reason for not going for a straightforward conspiracy theory about Conspiracy Theories.

The subtler reason is that a claim can be propaganda even if the people making it believe that it's true. Imagine a hypothetical Sandy Hook Conspiracy Theorist who really believes that the whole thing was a false flag operation by the government. He really believes his own propaganda, but that doesn't mean that it isn't propaganda. As the philosopher Jason Stanley points out in his book *How Propaganda Works*, propaganda can be sincere. Hitler's claims about the Jews were propaganda despite being sincere.[5]

In what sense are sincerely believed Conspiracy Theories propaganda? Think again about the idea that Conspiracy Theories are political gambits whose real function is to promote a political agenda. This is a technical use of 'function' that an analogy might help to make a bit clearer. Take an organ like the heart. If someone wants to know what the heart is, then a good way to explain it is to say that the heart is the organ responsible for pumping blood. That is its *function* or *purpose*. You explain what the thing is by explaining what it does, what it's for.

---

[5] Jason Stanley, *How Propaganda Works* (Princeton University Press, 2015), p. 45.

The (Real) Point of Conspiracy Theories

The same goes for Conspiracy Theories. The way to understand what they are is to understand what they are for, to grasp their basic function. Their basic function is to advance a political or ideological objective, be it opposition to gun control, anti-Semitism, hostility to the federal government or whatever. Conspiracy Theories advance a political objective in a special way: by advancing seductive explanations of major events that, objectively speaking, are unlikely to be true but *are* likely to influence public opinion in the preferred direction.

However, there is no need to assume that Conspiracy Theorists don't believe their own theories. The deluded Sandy Hook Conspiracy Theorist who sincerely believes that the whole thing was a hoax will be no less effective at getting the anti-gun control message across than an insincere proponent of the same view. Indeed, he might be *more* effective because he actually believes what he is saying. But the sincerity of the person who believes his own Conspiracy Theory doesn't mean that what he says isn't propaganda. Whatever his intentions, the actual function of his theory is to promote a political agenda by spreading what is in fact (whether he realises it or not) a bunch of seductive falsehoods.

The (Real) Point of Conspiracy Theories

When people think about propaganda, they usually have in mind the conscious and deliberate manipulation of public opinion by the spreading of falsehoods ('fake news'), half-truths or misleading images and stories. There *are* Conspiracy Theories that are propaganda in that sense – theories that deny the reality of the Holocaust are a case in point – but not all propaganda is like that and not all Conspiracy Theories are like that. There is also the unwitting propaganda of the deluded but sincere Sandy Hook Conspiracy Theorist (if such a person exists). What is or isn't propaganda isn't determined just by the intentions of the people who spread it. It is the fact that what they are spreading *is* fake news, together with the actual ideological associations and political implications of their stories and theories, that makes it propaganda.

Clearly there are Conspiracy Theories that have little or no political content. Perhaps theories about the death of Elvis are like that. To call them political propaganda would be silly. But that's not to deny that many of the most widely discussed Conspiracy Theories are overtly or covertly political. Even Conspiracy Theories about the moon landings are political. If the landings were faked, then who faked them? The government, presumably, or agents of the deep state, the Conspiracy Theorists' favourite multipurpose villain. Yet the minute one starts to talk about the secret, nefarious activities of the government or its agents, one is in the realm of politics and political propaganda. In the world of Conspiracy Theories politics is virtually inescapable.

The politics of many Conspiracy Theories is right-wing. When you look back at the history of Conspiracy Theories from the eighteenth century on, you can't fail to be struck by the extent to which they are underpinned by right-wing anti-Semitism. In one of the best books on the subject Jovan Byford comments that, 'for a substantial portion of its history, the conspiracy tradition was dominated by the idea of a Jewish plot to take over the world'.[6] Of course Conspiracy Theories don't have to be anti-Semitic. Nevertheless, it's striking how often in the world of Conspiracy Theories 'the Jews' are identified as the conspirators, either explicitly or in code.

There's no better example of a right-wing anti-Semitic Conspiracy Theory than the *Protocols of the Elders of Zion*, a notorious forgery that was first published in 1903. The *Protocols* supposedly

---

[6] Jovan Byford, *Conspiracy Theories: A Critical Introduction* (Palgrave Macmillan, 2011), p. 95.

describe a secret meeting at which a member of a group of Jewish elders outlines a fiendish plot for world domination. The full story of the text of the *Protocols* is told by the historian Norman Cohn.[7] Cohn describes how the alleged protocols were used to justify the massacres of Jews during the Russian Civil War and became an integral part of Nazi ideology. Quoted approvingly by Hitler in *Mein Kampf*, they helped to prepare the way for the Holocaust, at least according to Cohn.

Conspiracy Theories are as popular with the extreme left as they are with the extreme right. Hitler was a Conspiracy Theorist; but so was Stalin. Political extremism of one sort or another is the lifeblood of modern Conspiracy Theories. Right-wing theories target Jews, non-existent secret societies such as the Illuminati, and international organisations such as the United Nations and the Bilderberg Group. Left-wing theories tend to be anti-capitalist and anti-American. Some are anti-Semitic. Left and right are also in agreement about some other things, such as (in the US context) the evils of the federal government and its agencies.

---

[7] In his book *Warrant for Genocide: The Myth of the Jewish World Conspiracy and the Protocols of the Elders of Zion* (Serif, 1996).

That is one of the core themes of 9/11 Conspiracy Theories, which are as popular on the left as they are on the right.

Conspiracy Theories about the assassination of President Kennedy start to make more sense when viewed through the lens of practical politics and propaganda. Kennedy's lone assassin was Lee Harvey Oswald. Once memorably described as the 'loser's loser', Oswald was a self-proclaimed pro-Castro communist who had emigrated to the Soviet Union and tried to murder the right-wing politician Edwin Walker.[8] Yet after Oswald's own murder at the hands of night-club owner Jack Ruby elements on the left of American politics tried to shift the blame for the Kennedy assassination away from him and onto the deep state, the Mafia, or an unholy alliance of the two. In the same way, figures on the left and on the right have both found it convenient to shift the blame for 9/11 away from Al Qaeda and onto the Bush administration.

Conspiracy Theorists will no doubt claim that my description of their theories as political propaganda is itself political propaganda. It's one thing to accuse Conspiracy Theories of being political

---

[8] Robert Stone, 'The loser's loser', *New York Review of Books*, 22 June 1995.

propaganda if they are unlikely to be true, but why assume that Conspiracy Theories are unlikely to be true? Isn't the theory that Conspiracy Theories are fake news itself a blatant example of fake news designed to silence political dissents?

The assumption that Conspiracy Theories are unlikely to be true can be justified by taking a closer look at what makes them special. Theories about conspiracies can be true, and many are, but the special features of Conspiracy Theories don't do much for their chances of getting things right. Once you give up on the idea that Conspiracy Theories are there to tell the truth, there has to be another explanation of what they are up to.

One special feature of Conspiracy Theories that makes them different from other accounts of conspiracies is that they are *speculative*. By 'speculative' I mean that they are based on conjecture rather than knowledge, educated (or not so educated) guesswork rather than solid evidence. After all, if a conspiracy has been successful, then it won't have left behind evidence of a conspiracy. So the only way to uncover a conspiracy is by focusing on odd clues or anomalies that give the game away. Even clever conspirators make mistakes. Some things don't quite fit, and that is the Conspiracy Theorist's best hope. It's all about connecting the dots.

The (Real) Point of Conspiracy Theories

The best way to get a handle on the speculative nature of Conspiracy Theories is to do a comparison with a non-speculative theory about a conspiracy. A nice example is Operation Northwoods, as described by James Bamford.[9] It's an amazing but true story and an object lesson in the skulduggery of governments and their agencies.

Operation Northwoods was the code name of an operation dreamt up in 1962 by the chairman of the Joint Chiefs of Staff, General Lyman Lemnitzer. Lemnitzer, a rabidly right-wing Castro hater, wanted to give the Kennedy administration a pretext for invading Cuba. The pretext was to be a classic false flag operation: a series of terrorist attacks on the US mainland that would be blamed on Cuba. The phony evidence of Cuban involvement would give the general and his cronies in the military the excuse they needed to attack Cuba.

Lemnitzer's plan was never acted on and only came to light in 1997, when a memo describing the operation was made public by the John F. Kennedy Assassination Records Review Board. The document is now available on the National Security

---

[9] In his book *Body of Secrets: How America's NSA and Britain's GCHQ Eavesdrop on the World* (Arrow Books, 2002).

Archive and is well worth a read if you've never come across it.[10] Even after all these years it has the power to shock. But it does answer what would otherwise be an obvious question: how do we know that Operation Northwoods was ever planned? We know it was planned because the plans are there in black and white.

The story of Operation Northwoods is the story of a conspiracy and it's not in serious dispute that the story is genuine. Given that the story has the backing of unambiguous documentary evidence, it isn't speculative; it isn't a matter of *conjecture* what Lemnitzer was up to. There are no dots to connect; they're already connected in publicly available documents. And that's the difference between the story of Operation Northwoods and a Conspiracy Theory. There is nothing like the Northwoods memo to prove that 9/11 was an inside job, or that Oswald didn't kill Kennedy unassisted, or that Sandy Hook was a false flag operation. The story of Operation Northwoods isn't a Conspiracy Theory; it's conspiracy fact. Genuine Conspiracy Theories are speculative in a way that Bamford's account of Operation Northwoods is not. That's why they are *theories*.

---

[10] Visit https://nsarchive2.gwu.edu/news/20010430.

The (Real) Point of Conspiracy Theories

The view that Conspiracy Theories are speculative is sometimes expressed by saying that they may or may not be true; they have 'not yet been proven'.[11] But saying that Conspiracy Theories have not yet been proven is risky. It implies that they *could* yet be proven, but that can't be right if some Conspiracy Theories have already been disproved. The theory that the Holocaust was a myth is one that has been disproved about as conclusively as any theory could be. It's not a theory that 'may or may not be true'. So 'speculative' as I understand it is compatible with 'already disproved'.

Another key feature of Conspiracy Theories is that they are, as Rob Brotherton describes them, 'contrarian by nature'.[12] There's more than one way for that to be true. One way is to be contrary to the official view if there is one. The most well-known Conspiracy Theories are contrarian in this sense. They see the official view as part of the establishment's attempt to cover up the very conspiracy that the Conspiracy Theorist is trying to expose. If 'contrarian' means contrary to the official view then

---

[11] See Kathryn S. Olmsted, *Real Enemies: Conspiracy Theories and American Democracy, World War I to 9/11* (Oxford University Press, 2009), p. 3.
[12] Brotherton, *Suspicious Minds*, p. 68.

it's hard to imagine anything more contrarian than the theory than 9/11 was an inside job.

A complication is that governments themselves often peddle theories about conspiracies. President Bush's insistence that Iraq was involved in 9/11 is a good example of that, so why not call his theory a Conspiracy Theory even if it *was* the official view rather than one contrary to it? If Conspiracy Theories can be officially sanctioned, then they aren't necessarily contrarian. It seems arbitrary to deny that a theory about a conspiracy is a Conspiracy Theory simply because the government is behind it.

But there's a different sense in which Conspiracy Theories *are* always contrarian. The thing that Conspiracy Theories are contrary to is *appearances* or the *obvious* explanation of events. The whole point of a false flag operation is to do one thing while making it appear that something else happened. So the starting point of a Conspiracy Theory is that things aren't as they seem. The government agents who supposedly brought down the twin towers on 9/11 wouldn't have done a very good job if they hadn't made it look like Al Qaeda did it. So blaming 9/11 on the government is tantamount to saying that there is a fundamental mismatch between how things look and how they are.

The (Real) Point of Conspiracy Theories

Why are Conspiracy Theorists so confident that things aren't as they seem? Why are they so confident that the government was responsible for 9/11, given the mountains of evidence that Al Qaeda did it? Because they think that aircraft impacts and the resulting fires couldn't have brought down the twin towers. 'Couldn't have' means 'it isn't physically possible for such a thing to have happened'. In the same way, Conspiracy Theories about the assassination of President Kennedy say that a single bullet couldn't have caused all the injuries to the president and to Governor Connally, who was riding with him in the presidential limousine when the fatal shots were fired. On the other hand, school shooting Conspiracy Theories don't deny that a lone gunman *could* have been responsible. They question the reality of the shooting rather than its possibility.

When Conspiracy Theories talk about what is or isn't physically possible, they rely – or claim to rely – on science. When someone argues that X didn't happen because it's not possible, the obvious reply is: 'well, X *did* happen, so X is possible'. Aircraft impacts *did* cause the twin towers to fall, so it was possible for them to do so. The science that is supposed to prove that aircraft impacts couldn't have brought down the towers, or that a single bullet couldn't have caused all the injuries that President Kennedy and Governor Connally suffered, is controversial. Most of the officially sanctioned experts take a different view. The question is, which experts should we trust? The only ones that Conspiracy Theorists are prepared to trust are other Conspiracy Theorists.

The fact that Conspiracy Theories reject the obvious explanation of events such as 9/11 and are so keen on the idea of a mismatch between appearance and reality gives their theories an esoteric feel. That's another special feature of Conspiracy Theories. Once the obvious is ruled out and the far from obvious is ruled in, the Conspiracy Theorist's imagination can and usually does run wild. There is almost no explanation that isn't too bizarre for the Conspiracy Theorist's taste – apart, that is, from the obvious one. If how things are isn't how they look, who is to say how strange the actual truth is?

An amusing example of the Conspiracy Theorist's almost insatiable taste for the esoteric is Richard H. Popkin's account of the Kennedy assassination.[13] The official view is that Oswald shot Kennedy without help from anyone else. But blaming Oswald is too easy for Popkin. He has other ideas,

---

[13] Richard H. Popkin, *The Second Oswald* (Boson Books, 2008).

including the belief that the shooting was the work of a 'Second Oswald', a man who looked like Oswald but wasn't him. That's one of a long list of theories that Popkin is willing to contemplate. The more esoteric the theory, the greater its appeal to Conspiracy Theorists.

Popkin has a lot to say in his book about forensics and ballistics. Conspiracy buffs will know that questions about the trajectory of the bullets fired by Oswald and the wounds suffered by Kennedy and Connally have played a major part in debates about the assassination. Popkin isn't shy about weighing in on these issues. Yet he was no forensic scientist and had no proven expertise in wound ballistics, the scientific study of the effects of high-velocity projectiles on human tissue. Who, then, was Popkin, and what were his credentials for pontificating on these matters? He was, in fact, a professor of philosophy whose most famous work was a history of scepticism from Erasmus to Descartes.

If one were looking for a single word to describe the nature of Popkin's interest in the Kennedy assassination, that word would be 'amateur'. And that's another feature of Conspiracy Theories. They are, by and large, amateurish. That's not a comment on their intellectual merits, but on the qualifications of the amateur sleuths and Internet detectives who push them. One of the most famous 9/11 Conspiracy Theorists, David Ray Griffin, was professor of philosophy of religion at the Claremont School of Theology in California. James Fetzer made his name as a philosopher of science based at the University of Minnesota in Duluth. Questions about the nature and merits of Conspiracy Theories are certainly philosophical (that's my excuse for writing this book); questions about the technical merits of individual Conspiracy Theories are not.

Philosophers aren't the only amateurs who weigh in on individual Conspiracy Theories. The contributors to a 2007 book on 9/11 Conspiracy Theories edited by Fetzer include a retired professor of economics, a professor of English, and a chief executive officer.[14] Some 9/11 Conspiracy Theorists do have qualifications in relevant subjects such as mechanical engineering, but they are in a small minority. Besides, having a degree in a relevant subject doesn't mean that one's opinions have greater validity than those of countless mainstream experts in the same field who don't buy into Conspiracy Theories.

---

[14] J. Fetzer (ed.), *The 9/11 Conspiracy: The Scamming of America* (Catfeet Press, 2007).

The (Real) Point of Conspiracy Theories

The amateurishness of many Conspiracy Theories has some strange consequences. Conspiracy Theorists who are quick to denounce mainstream academia for rejecting their theories nevertheless crave academic respectability. They set up pseudo-academic journals for the study of this or that alleged conspiracy and trumpet their PhDs, whatever their subject. They have a particular fondness for footnotes.[15] As Jovan Byford notes, the footnote is so valuable to the amateur Conspiracy Theorist because it creates the impression that his theories are the product of reliable research into trustworthy sources. It's a pity, then, that these trustworthy sources turn out to be, for the most part, other Conspiracy Theorists.

There's one more special feature of Conspiracy Theories that's worth noting. It's a feature identified in an article on conspiracy theories by the philosopher Brian Keeley.[16] If nothing else, the article proves that not all philosophers who write about Conspiracy Theories are Conspiracy Theorists.

---

[15] For example, David Ray Griffin's *The New Pearl Harbor: Disturbing Questions about the Bush Administration and 9/11* (Arris Books, 2004) has some two hundred pages of text followed by some fifty pages of notes.

[16] Brian Keeley, 'Of conspiracy theories', *Journal of Philosophy* 96 (1999): 109–26.

The (Real) Point of Conspiracy Theories

Conspiracy Theories, Keeley cogently argues, embody a thoroughly outdated worldview and a perspective on the meaning of life that was more appropriate in the last century (by which he means the nineteenth century; Keeley's article was published in 1999). The worldview that Keeley describes is premodern. It is the view that complex events are capable of being controlled by a small number of people acting in secret, and this is what gives these events a deeper meaning. From this perspective, things always happen for a reason.

It's true, of course, that things sometimes happen for a reason – but not the reasons cited by Conspiracy Theories. Kennedy died for a reason: Oswald decided to shoot him and had the skill or luck to do it. But why did Oswald decide to murder Kennedy in the first place? And why was Oswald himself shot by Jack Ruby while in police custody? From a modern (as distinct from premodern) perspective, all we can really say is: shit happens.[17] People do crazy things and there are limits to our ability to make sense of their actions. In these cases, there is no deeper meaning to be found and there are no all-powerful hidden conspirators pulling the strings.

---

[17] P. Mandik, 'Shit happens', *Episteme: The Journal of Social Epistemology* 4 (2007): 205–18.

The (Real) Point of Conspiracy Theories

The same goes for 9/11. Of course, that *was* a conspiracy, an Al Qaeda conspiracy. It's hard in retrospect to grasp its enormity and the huge slices of luck that were needed for Mohammad Atta and his fellow hijackers to pull off their operation. They certainly made mistakes and the authorities missed many opportunities to foil the plot. Why were these opportunities missed? It didn't help that the FBI and the CIA were at loggerheads about Al Qaeda. If they had been more collaborative, they might have been able to stop the attacks. But there is no deeper meaning to the fact that they didn't collaborate. It's just how large bureaucracies work. Petty personal and institutional rivalries can have devastating consequences.[18]

It's time to take stock. I began by arguing that a Conspiracy Theory isn't just any old theory about a conspiracy. Conspiracy Theories have a bunch of special features that make them different from many other theories about conspiracies, such as the theory that Guy Fawkes and others conspired to blow up parliament in 1605 or the theory that the Joint Chiefs of Staff conspired against Cuba in 1962. More controversially, I suggested that

---

[18] These rivalries are described by L. Wright in *The Looming Tower: Al-Qaeda's Road to 9/11* (Penguin Books, 2011).

it's precisely these special features of Conspiracy Theories that make them unlikely to be true. This is why it makes sense to think of such theories as forms of propaganda. Once you've given up on the idea that their point is to tell the truth, a different account of their function is called for.

Here, then, is my list of what makes Conspiracy Theories special. As I've tried to explain, these theories are speculative, contrarian, esoteric, amateurish and premodern. This isn't an exhaustive list and I'll mention another special feature in chapter 4. But, if we stick to the current list, several things should now be clear. First, it should be clear why well-documented accounts of events like the Gunpowder Plot and Operation Northwoods aren't Conspiracy Theories; they lack at least the first four of my five features. There is nothing speculative, contrarian or esoteric about mainstream historical accounts of the Gunpowder Plot; and the people writing these accounts aren't amateurs. They are called historians.

The second thing that should now be clear is why widely discussed Conspiracy Theories about events like 9/11 really are Conspiracy Theories and not just theories about conspiracies. They have all the special features of Conspiracy Theories. The theory that governments agents somehow managed to plant explosives in the twin towers in advance of 9/11 and to detonate them just when the planes hit is speculative by anyone's lights, contrarian in every reasonable sense, and highly esoteric. Most of the people proposing this theory are amateurs and there is no doubt that their theory invests 9/11 with a meaning or significance it wouldn't otherwise have.

However, the most important point is this: theories that have all five of the special features of Conspiracy Theories that I've listed are *unlikely* to be true even if it is *possible* for them to be true. From the fact that a theory is speculative it doesn't follow that it is false. From the fact that a theory is contrarian or esoteric it doesn't follow that it is false either. Amateurs can and do sometimes discover truths missed by professionals. And sometimes major events do have a deeper meaning. But now put all these things together and you have a type of theory that is unlikely to be true. That's why we aren't justified in believing Conspiracy Theories. They aren't credible.

It's easy enough to see why speculative theories are much less likely to be true than non-speculative theories. Theories that are based on conjecture rather than solid evidence are doomed to be wrong more often than not. Of course, Conspiracy Theorists think that they have solid evidence in support of their theories, but it's in the nature of Conspiracy Theories to rely on circumstantial rather than direct evidence. The perfect conspiracy is one that leaves no trace and is therefore unknowable. In that sense, there's always a tension between the Conspiracy Theorist's view of the supposed conspirators as ingenious and all-powerful and his confidence in his own ability to outfox them. If the conspirators are so clever, how come they have been rumbled by a bunch of amateurs? Or have they?

Are contrarian and esoteric explanations less likely to be true than conformist and mundane ones? That depends on what one thinks reality is like. If truth is stranger than fiction, then that would be a case for going against appearances and settling for the esoteric. But what if, as seems much more likely, fiction is stranger than truth? In that case, always assuming that things aren't as they seem won't be an effective explanatory strategy. Human conduct is sometimes unfathomable; but, when it isn't, the best explanations are remarkably mundane. You don't need a conspiracy to explain why the CIA screwed up over 9/11, just some basic knowledge of how large bureaucracies work. As good an explanation as any of Oswald's actions in Dallas is his well-documented desire for fame. He succeeded not because anyone else was helping him but because, as his army records show, he was a good shot.

When all these factors are added to the amateur status of most Conspiracy Theorists, there is only one possible conclusion: Conspiracy Theories could be true but are unlikely to be. But that doesn't matter if, as I've been arguing, their primary function is to promote a political or ideological agenda rather than to tell the truth. In practice what counts is not whether a Conspiracy Theory is true, but whether it is seductive. On that score it's hard to question the success of many Conspiracy Theories. They tell stories that people want to hear.

Whether these stories are really believed or not is sometimes hard to say. The fact that a person retweets a Conspiracy Theory doesn't necessarily mean that he believes it. But there is no doubt that people find Conspiracy Theories intriguing enough to want to circulate them, discuss them and think about them. Why is that? This is where some psychologists see an opening. They want to explain the popularity of Conspiracy Theories, and of course they want to explain it in psychological terms. This brings us to my next question. Are psychological explanations of Conspiracy Theories any good? That's a question that deserves its own chapter.

2

Why Are Conspiracy Theories So Popular?

Just how popular *are* Conspiracy Theories? It's sometimes suggested that we are living in a 'golden age' of Conspiracy Theories, but it's actually not clear that Conspiracy Theories are a hotter topic today than in the past. In their book *American Conspiracy Theories*, political scientists Joseph Uscinski and Joseph Parent describe the results of a fascinating study of conspiracy talk in letters sent to the *New York Times* between 1890 and 2010.[1] Perhaps surprisingly, they found that discussion of conspiracy theories has *diminished* in the United States since 1890. At least as far as America is concerned, we don't live in an age of conspiracy theories.

---

[1] *American Conspiracy Theories* (Oxford University Press, 2014).

Why Are Conspiracy Theories So Popular?

Conspiracy talk comes in several varieties. On the one hand, there is the conspiracy talk of people who invent Conspiracy Theories, usually in order to circulate them more widely and to get other people to buy into them. You might think of individuals who come up with Conspiracy Theories as Conspiracy Theory *producers*. On the other hand, if all you do is consume other people's theories, then you are a Conspiracy Theory *consumer* rather than a producer. There are many different ways of 'consuming' a theory – any theory. For example, you can consume it by discussing it with friends, by posting something about it on Facebook or by retweeting it. All it takes to consume a Conspiracy Theory is to engage with it actively, one way or another.

Given the distinction between producing and consuming, the obvious next question is: why do producers produce Conspiracy Theories and why do consumers consume them? You might think that this obvious question has an equally obvious answer: producers produce and promote Conspiracy Theories because they believe their theories to be *true*. And the same goes for consumers of Conspiracy Theories: the theories they consume are ones that they *believe in*.

It doesn't take long to work out that this can't be right; there are plenty of reasons for producing or consuming Conspiracy Theories that have little or nothing to do with belief in their truth. For a start, it's worth bearing in mind that Conspiracy Theories are big business and it wouldn't be too surprising if that has something to do with the willingness of some individuals to produce and promote such theories. These individuals aren't just Conspiracy Theory producers. They are also what Cass Sunstein calls *conspiracy entrepreneurs*, that is, conspiracy theorists who profit from promoting their theories.[2]

A good illustration of the business potential of Conspiracy Theories is the virtual store on Conspiracy Theorist Alex Jones's website Infowars. The range of products for sale includes not only survival gear and other conspiracy-related products but also dietary supplements, 'male vitality' pills and toothpaste. The Conspiracy Theories for which Jones is famous (or infamous, depending on your point of view) are a marketing opportunity as well as a political statement.

The point is not that Conspiracy Theory producers don't believe their own theories, though some of these are so outlandish that one has to wonder

---

[2] Cass Sunstein, *Conspiracy Theories and Other Dangerous Ideas* (Simon & Schuster, 2014), p. 12.

whether they are serious. Does Alex Jones mean what he says about Sandy Hook being a false flag? Probably. Is David Icke serious about the planet's being ruled by shape-shifting reptilians? Who can say? But one thing is clear: there's good money to be made by peddling such theories.

If this seems a little unfair on Conspiracy Theorists, perhaps it's worth pointing out that one of their favourite questions is *Cui bono?* – that is, 'Who benefits?'. For example, the theory that 9/11 was an inside job appeals to them partly because they think that the Bush administration benefited from the attacks. But if it's fair to ask who benefits from events such as 9/11, then it's also fair to ask who benefits from Conspiracy Theories about such events. And the answer in many cases appears to be: the very people who produce and promote these theories.

The benefits that Conspiracy Theories bring to their producers aren't just financial. If, as I've suggested, Conspiracy Theories can be an effective way of promoting a political ideology or of achieving a political objective, then that's another potential benefit. Belief in the literal truth of Conspiracy Theories needn't come into it if they are a form of political propaganda. You don't have to believe that Sandy Hook was a false flag in order to spread the story that it was, as a way of combating calls for greater gun control in the wake of the shooting. In much the same way, anti-Semitic Conspiracy Theorists have frequently invented and circulated anti-Semitic Conspiracy Theories that they knew to be false. It's enough to think of whoever came up with the *Protocols of the Elders of Zion*.

It's even more obvious that consumers of Conspiracy Theories don't have to believe them. There are plenty of ways of actively engaging with a Conspiracy Theory you don't endorse. One way is, of course, to argue against it, and people engaging in 'conspiracy talk' include both opponents and proponents of Conspiracy Theories. Some people talk about Conspiracy Theories because they find them intriguing or entertaining. Posting details of a Conspiracy Theory on Facebook is a way of engaging with it, but it's not unusual – to put it mildly – for people to post things on social media that they don't necessarily think are true. The extent to which people are agnostic about Conspiracy Theories is just as striking as the extent to which these theories are actively supported or opposed.

Still, there's no denying that significant numbers of people – producers and consumers – *do* believe, or say they believe, at least one prominent Conspiracy Theory. A study five years after 9/11 found that more than a third of Americans believed that the government had either assisted in the attacks or knew about them in advance and did nothing to stop them. A more recent study found that 63 per cent of registered voters in the United States buy into at least one conspiracy theory (or, in my terminology, one Conspiracy Theory). And, of course, it isn't just Americans who are into Conspiracy Theories. These are also prevalent in other parts of the world, and it's often said that the Middle East is a particular hotspot for belief in Conspiracy Theories.

From a psychological perspective, the number of people who seemingly endorse one or more Conspiracy Theories calls for a psychological explanation. Hence the birth of a new field of study: the psychology of Conspiracy Theories. Needless to say, Conspiracy Theorists haven't been keen on being studied by psychologists and it's not difficult to understand their lack of enthusiasm. Their position is, of course, that their theories are based on evidence and that no psychological explanation is called for. If a person has good evidence that 9/11 was an inside job, then that is usually enough to explain why that person believes that 9/11 was an inside job. What has psychology got to do with it?

What Conspiracy Theorists who argue like this are picking up on is a strange feature of many discussions of Conspiracy Theories from a psychological viewpoint. These discussions often start by saying that they take no position as to the actual truth or falsity of Conspiracy Theories. The psychologist's concern, they insist, is not whether these theories are true or false but why people believe them.

To see how odd this is, imagine a psychology of bananas. Specialists in this imaginary field say that they take no position on the actual existence of bananas. Their concern is not whether the widespread belief in the existence of bananas is true or false but only why people have this belief. However, the obvious explanation of a belief in the existence of bananas isn't neutral as to their existence. The obvious explanation is that people believe that bananas exist because bananas *do* exist and most of us know perfectly well that they do. The implication of asking why people believe X is that there is something *wrong* with believing X. This implication doesn't hold in a case where X stands for *bananas*, and that's why the whole idea of a psychology of bananas is so weird.

Conspiracy Theories aren't (literally) bananas, but asking why people believe them implies that those people are at fault for believing them. It implies, for example, that there is no legitimate reason to believe Conspiracy Theories. This is the implication that Conspiracy Theorists object to, and that many psychologists try to avoid. But there is no avoiding it. There is no neutral standpoint from which it makes sense to ask why people believe Conspiracy Theories. Either there is nothing wrong with believing them, in which case the question doesn't arise, or the question does arise, in which case there is something wrong with believing them.

Given that Conspiracy Theories are unlikely to be true and a good number of them have been conclusively refuted, it's reasonable to ask why people still believe them. Whether this reasonable question is one to which psychology gives a reasonable answer remains to be seen. It would be rash to deny that psychology has anything useful to say about this, but psychological accounts of belief in Conspiracy Theories are incomplete in one crucial respect: they don't pay nearly enough attention to the role of politics.

If you read what psychologists have to say about belief in Conspiracy Theories, you'll probably come away with two insights. One is that Conspiracy Theories have something to do with the way our brains work. As Rob Brotherton puts it, these theories result from 'some of our brain's quirks and foibles', including some of our brain's inbuilt biases and shortcuts.[3]

The other insight from psychology is that belief in Conspiracy Theories is at least partly a question of personality: there are measurable individual differences in how willing people are to accept such theories. People who have a propensity to believe them are described as having a 'conspiracy mentality' or as being 'conspiracy-minded'. Psychologists have even devised a Conspiracy Mentality Scale (in psychology there's always a scale). On this view, being conspiracy-minded is a personality trait, and knowing that a person is highly conspiracy-minded enables one to predict his response to a Conspiracy Theory he hasn't come across before. The more conspiracy-minded he is, the more likely he is to believe a new Conspiracy Theory.

When psychologists talk about our brain's 'quirks and foibles', they're usually talking about a range of so-called cognitive biases. Here are three of them:

- intentionality bias – the tendency to assume that things happen because they were intended rather than accidental;

[3] Rob Brotherton, *Suspicious Minds: Why We Believe Conspiracy Theories* (Bloomsbury Sigma, 2015), p. 17.

- confirmation bias – the tendency to look only for evidence that supports what one already believes while ignoring contrary evidence;
- proportionality bias – the tendency to assume that the scale of an event's cause must match the scale of the event itself.

Of course, some things *do* happen because somebody intended them to happen and big effects *do* sometimes have big causes. But assuming that this is always the case will sometimes lead one astray.

It's easy to see how biases related to intentionality and proportionality might play a part in generating some Conspiracy Theories, while confirmation bias helps to sustain preexisting theories. Take the disappearance of flight MH-370. When Malaysia Airlines flight 370 disappeared without trace in March 2014, many explanations were put forward. Was it an accident? Quite possibly, but Conspiracy Theorists have other ideas: the pilot and the co-pilot deliberately crashed the plane, it was brought down by a missile, it was hijacked, it was the victim of a cyberattack, and so on. Take your pick, but what all these explanations have in common is the assumption that MH-370 vanished because somebody intended it. That's intentionality bias in action.

Proportionality bias has been blamed for Conspiracy Theories about the assassination of JFK. If big effects must have correspondingly big causes, then it's not surprising that Conspiracy Theorists have a hard time accepting that somebody as insignificant as Oswald could have been responsible for the death of a president. So either he wasn't as insignificant as he seems or other people were involved. And, once proportionality bias has generated a Conspiracy Theory about the assassination, confirmation bias keeps the theory going. The search for decisive evidence of a conspiracy is ongoing, while the decisive evidence that Oswald killed Kennedy without help from anyone else is downplayed or ignored.

Attractive as cognitive bias explanations of Conspiracy Theories might appear, there is an obvious problem with them: cognitive biases are universal – they affect all of us – but belief in Conspiracy Theories is not. How is it, then, that many people seemingly *aren't* Conspiracy Theorists? Do their brains work differently from the brains of Conspiracy Theorists? That's not an inference that psychologists have been prepared to draw. What they argue instead is that, to quote Brotherton again, 'we are all natural-born conspiracy theorists'.[4]

---

[4] Ibid.

Why Are Conspiracy Theories So Popular?

It's undeniable that we all believe some conspiracy theories with a small 'c' and a small 't', that is, some accounts of conspiracies. But that's not the issue. The issue is whether we are all prone to believing Conspiracy Theories with a capital 'C' and a capital 'T'. That's unlikely. I have no urge to believe that 9/11 was an inside job, that Sandy Hook was a false flag or that Oswald didn't act alone in assassinating JFK. I'm not a Conspiracy Theorist and I don't think I'm unique in this regard. We aren't all Conspiracy Theorists, let alone natural-born Conspiracy Theorists.

It would be nice but probably unrealistic to think that non-Conspiracy Theorists are somehow immune to cognitive biases or in general less susceptible to them than Conspiracy Theorists. Of course, belief in Conspiracy Theories – like belief in anything else – has something to do with the way our brains work, but the quirks and foibles of the human brain don't look like a good bet when it comes to explaining beliefs that only a minority of human beings – albeit a significant minority – have.

What about the idea of conspiracy mindedness as a personality trait? This looks much more promising, since there is no suggestion that everybody has this trait. Psychologists point to evidence that people who believe one conspiracy theory (one Conspiracy

Theory as I would put it) are more likely to believe other such theories, even totally unrelated ones. Isn't that proof that belief in Conspiracy Theories has more to do with the believer's personality than with the rational assessment of the evidence?

In one of the most influential academic discussions of conspiracy theories, Ted Goertzel argued that conspiratorial beliefs typically make up what he dubbed a *monological* belief system.[5] In a monological belief system, each belief supports every other belief, and the more conspiracies a monological thinker believes in the more likely he or she is to believe in any new conspiracy theory, regardless of its subject matter. For example, if you believe that 9/11 was an inside job, then you are more likely to believe a Conspiracy Theory about Princess Diana's death in a car crash. Yet there is no obvious connection between these theories.

Goertzel's idea was put to the test in a study by Michael Wood, Karen Douglas and Robbie Sutton.[6] They found that people who subscribe to a bunch of conspiracy theories are not only more likely to

[5] T. Goertzel, 'Belief in conspiracy theories', *Political Psychology* 15 (1994): 731–42.

[6] M. Wood, K. Douglas and R. Sutton, 'Dead and alive: Belief in contradictory conspiracy theories', *Social Psychological and Personality Science* 3 (2012): 767–73.

subscribe to other, *unrelated* conspiracy theories, they are also prepared to sign up to *contradictory* theories. People who believe that Princess Diana faked her own death (and hence is still alive) are significantly more likely to believe that she was murdered (and hence is dead) by enemies of her boyfriend's father, Mohammed Al-Fayed. The more the participants in the study believed that Osama bin Laden was already dead when American Special Forces raided his compound in Abbottabad, the more they believed that he is still alive.

Psychological studies like this should always come with a health warning. Their guinea pigs are almost always undergraduates studying psychology, and so are hardly representative of the general population. There are also concerns about whether their findings can be reproduced in matching studies. Still, taking the psychological evidence at face value, it's hard not to draw the conclusion that there is such a thing as being conspiracy-minded or having a conspiracy *mindset* that predisposes you to believe conspiracy theories.

What psychological studies *don't* prove is that being conspiracy-minded is a personality trait. A different interpretation of the evidence is that the conspiracy mindset is an *ideology* rather than a personality trait. An ideology is a set of fundamental ideas and beliefs that shape one's understanding of political reality. For example, Marxism is an ideology in this sense, and so is what is sometimes referred to as 'conspiracism'. Fundamental to conspiracism is the belief that people in authority are hiding things from the rest of us as part of a conspiracy to achieve their own sinister goals. If this is what you believe, then it's understandable if you end up endorsing even contradictory theories, as long as they are all in keeping with your overall conspiracist ideology.

What's the difference between an ideology and a personality trait? Personality traits as generally understood by psychologists aren't ideas or beliefs, whatever else they are. For example, one of the so-called Big Five personality traits is *agreeableness*, but being agreeable isn't a matter of believing anything in particular. In contrast, being conspiracy-minded *is* a matter of believing something in particular: it's a matter of believing that people in authority are hiding things from the rest of us. In addition, personality traits have a genetic basis, but it's debatable whether ideologies like conspiracism are genetic. For these reasons it's safer to think of conspiracy mindedness as an ideology than as a personality trait.

The ideological interpretation of conspiracy mindedness explains another well-known result of psychological research. Viren Swami and his colleagues made up a conspiracy theory about the drink Red Bull and tried the theory out on 169 women and 112 men from Austria, where the brand is well known. Elements of the theory included the claim that Red Bull contains substances that raise desire for the product and that the advertising slogan 'Red Bull gives you wings' was chosen because, in testing, rats who were given the drink literally grew wings.[7]

The Red Bull study showed that the strongest predictor of belief in the fictitious conspiracy theory was belief in other real-world conspiracy theories. Again, this is just what one would expect if being conspiracy-minded is an ideology. A conspiracist has a general disposition to believe conspiracy theories, and this disposition can be strong enough to get him to believe entirely fictitious as well as contra-dictory Conspiracy Theories. His commitment to a conspiracist ideology trumps all other consid-erations and shapes his response to individual Conspiracy Theories.

Is that it, then? Do we now have an answer to the question of why people believe Conspiracy

---

[7] V. Swami et al., 'Conspiracist ideation in Britain and Austria', *British Journal of Psychology* 102 (2011): 443–63.

Why Are Conspiracy Theories So Popular?

Theories? Can we say that people believe Conspiracy Theories because they are conspiracy-minded, that is, committed to the ideology of conspiracism? We could say this, but only if we're prepared to answer a further question. Why are some people conspiracy-minded? Why are they committed to the ideology of conspiracism? Without an answer to this, all we get from psychology is the not very exciting insight that people believe Conspiracy Theories because, as a matter of ideology or personality, they are predisposed to believe Conspiracy Theories. A more complete explanation also needs to say *why* it is that some people have this predisposition.

Here's one possibility: the ideology of conspiracism is attractive to some because it fits their *broader* ideological or political commitments. Some political outlooks are more conducive to conspiracism than others. Among the political outlooks that are conducive to conspiracism, there are variations in the particular types of Conspiracy Theory they support. In the American context, for example, Uscinski and Parent suggest that liberals tend to be Truthers (i.e. to believe that President Bush was directly or indirectly responsible for the 9/11 attacks), whereas conservatives tend to be Birthers (i.e. to believe that President Obama wasn't born in America).

Why Are Conspiracy Theories So Popular?

Tying conspiracism to ideology in this way is a good way of building on the notion that Conspiracy Theories are forms of political propaganda. For propaganda to be effective, people need to believe it and the propaganda model needs to explain why Conspiracy Theories are believed by some of their consumers. It's not just a matter of these consumers having a general tendency to believe Conspiracy Theories. They're also inclined to accept *particular* Conspiracy Theories or particular *types* of Conspiracy Theory. Which ones? Ones that are in line with their political outlook. For example, people with free market ideologies are more likely to accept climate change Conspiracy Theories. Why would that be? Presumably because, as committed free marketeers, they don't like the regulations that would be needed to combat climate change if climate change is real.

What is true of Conspiracy Theory consumers is also true of Conspiracy Theory producers. The Conspiracy Theories they devise and promote are those that match their particular political or ideological commitments. To this extent ideology is both the cause and the effect of many Conspiracy Theories. On the one hand, it is a major part of what makes them attractive to some people in the first place. On the other hand, the political ideologies

49

that make them attractive are also the political ideologies that it is their function to promote.

The ideologies that are most conducive to Conspiracy Theories are extremist ideologies. In a study for the British think tank Demos, Jamie Bartlett and Carl Miller show that Conspiracy Theories are prevalent across the extremist spectrum.[8] Far-right ideologies often incorporate anti-Semitic Conspiracy Theories, and it should come as no surprise if right-wing extremists are vociferous Conspiracy Theorists. Left-wing Conspiracy Theorists focus on global elites and on international financiers. Since such groups are assumed by many on the left to be Jewish, left-wing Conspiracy Theories can be as anti-Semitic as right-wing Conspiracy Theories.

Another extremist political ideology with links to conspiracism is Islamism. According to Al Qaeda, for example, there is a Judeo-Christian conspiracy to destroy Islam. Osama bin Laden made many statements to this effect and it's more straightforward to see his conspiracism as a reflection of his Islamist ideology than as a personality trait. Islamist Conspiracy Theories are generally anti-Semitic. The official manifesto of Hamas, the Islamic Resistance

---

[8] J. Bartlett and C. Miller, *The Power of Unreason: Conspiracy Theories, Extremism and Counter-Terrorism* (Demos, 2010).

Movement in Gaza, even quotes the *Protocols of the Elders of Zion* as if they were genuine.

One worry about the hypothesis that the ideology of conspiracism has its roots in extremist ideologies such as fascism, communism or Islamism is that there are extremists who are not Conspiracy Theorists. If not *everyone* on the extreme left or extreme right is a Conspiracy Theorist, then how can the conspiracism of *anyone* on the extreme left or extreme right be adequately explained by his extremism? In the same way, Uscinski and Parent note that not all American liberals are Truthers and not all conservatives are Birthers. So, when confronted by a Birther who also happens to be a conservative, how can it possibly be right to explain his conspiracism by reference to his conservatism? Is there really a causal connection between conspiracism and politics in a more general sense?

Think of an analogy. Smoking, we are told, causes lung cancer. Yet lots of people who smoke don't get lung cancer. In fact, medical research suggests only around 17 per cent of current male smokers will get lung cancer.[9] So in what sense

---

[9] P. Villeneuve and Y. Mao, 'Lifetime probability of developing lung cancer, by smoking status, Canada', *Canadian Journal of Public Health* 85 (1994): 385–8.

does smoking cause lung cancer? If not *everyone* who smokes gets lung cancer, how can *any* smoker's lung cancer be adequately explained by the fact that he smoked? The answer is, because smoking significantly increases a person's chances of getting lung cancer. Maybe only 17 per cent of male smokers will eventually get lung cancer, but among non-smokers the figure is only just over 1 per cent. To say that smoking 'causes' lung cancer is to say that it is a major risk factor for lung cancer. If you want to reduce levels of lung cancer, it's a good idea to reduce levels of smoking. It's irrelevant that lots of smokers don't get lung cancer.

In much the same way, being committed to an extremist ideology is a significant risk factor for conspiracism. Even if not all fascists, communists or Islamists are conspiracy-minded, being committed to one of these ideologies significantly raises the probability that one will be a conspiracist. Why should that be? Because conspiracism is integral to these ideologies. This is clearest in the case of extreme right-wing or fascist ideologies such as the one espoused by Hitler in *Mein Kampf*. For these ideologies, conspiracism isn't an optional extra. It's part and parcel of their core vision, so one would expect people who buy into the core vision to buy into conspiracism.

Why Are Conspiracy Theories So Popular?

Rather than worrying about the fact that not all extremists are conspiracists, one might worry instead about the fact that not all conspiracists are extremists. Just as there are non-smokers who get lung cancer, there are people whose politics is middle-of-the-road but who are still conspiracists. In their case, conspiracism looks like a more free-standing political ideology, one that isn't obviously related to their other political commitments. How come they are still conspiracists? What other factors are at play?

It's helpful to think about this because, even in the case of people who *are* extremists of one sort or another, it would be naïve to suppose that their conspiracism is *wholly* explained by their other ideological or political commitments. Human beings aren't that simple, and one would expect a satisfactory explanation of a person's conspiracism to be complex rather than simple, multidimensional rather than one-dimensional. The challenge is to identify a *range* of factors that can lead to conspiracism, even among political moderates.

One important factor is the extent to which one is a member of a community that has been the victim of actual rather than imaginary conspiracies. For example, one finding of research into belief in Conspiracy Theories in the US context is that

Why Are Conspiracy Theories So Popular?

African Americans and Hispanics are more likely to be conspiracy-minded than white people. Popular conspiratorial beliefs among African Americans include the belief that AIDS was created to kill black people and that the federal government selectively flooded black neighbourhoods during Hurricane Katrina by blowing up the levees.

Even if these Conspiracy Theories are unlikely to be true, the actions they describe aren't any more horrifying than things that have actually been done to African Americans by successive governments. For example, in the aftermath of the Great Depression, the US Public Health Service decided to do a study of untreated syphilis among African American men. In what came to be known as the Tuskegee Experiment, around 600 impoverished sharecroppers were recruited and observed over several decades. Even when an effective treatment for syphilis was discovered, the study wasn't discontinued and the men weren't treated. The research only came to an end in 1972, when a whistle-blower leaked the story to the press. In 1997, President Bill Clinton apologised to victims of the experiment on behalf of the United States.

It's only to be expected that minority communities that have been victims of racist conspiracies like the Tuskegee Experiment are more conspiracy-minded than communities that haven't. They have good reason to be suspicious of government. It's a case of once bitten twice shy, and theories that might otherwise seem outlandish don't look all that implausible when viewed from the perspective of victim communities. If government agencies are capable of pulling a stunt like Tuskegee, why wouldn't they be capable of setting out to infect African Americans with AIDS?

One answer to this question is that the bad things that a government is capable of doing aren't necessarily things that it has actually done. There isn't good evidence in support of the AIDS Conspiracy Theory, and new regulations and safeguards that came into force after Tuskegee would make it difficult for government agencies to do anything similar again even if they wanted to. Still, the fact remains that the conspiracism of many African Americans has nothing to do with their personality *or* their political ideology. It's just an understandable reaction to how they have been treated.

The point is a general one. The more you learn about *proven* conspiracies in your part of the world, the more you will be inclined to believe *unproven* Conspiracy Theories. You might be receptive to Conspiracy Theories because of your other ideological commitments, but it's also possible that they have absolutely nothing to do with it. You don't have to be an extremist to be a Conspiracy Theorist, because you don't have to be an extremist to be a victim of a real conspiracy.

Nor do you have to be an extremist to be politically marginalised. That's worth pointing out, because political marginalisation is another factor that has been identified as making people more conspiracy-minded. One study tested the hypothesis that conspiracy interpretations of the world flourish in the context of marginalisation, poverty, and other negative life circumstances.[10] The results are striking. People who are conspiracy-minded are more likely to see themselves as being at the bottom of the social ladder, to have thought seriously about committing suicide, to have trouble sleeping, and to feel less able to rely on family or friends in the event of a crisis. The authors of the study are careful to point out that, just because there is a correlation between conspiracy mindedness and marginalisation, it doesn't follow that the two are causally connected. Even if they are connected, is it marginalisation that causes

---

[10] D. Freeman and R. Bentall, 'The concomitants of conspiracy concerns', *Social Psychiatry and Psychiatric Epidemiology* 52 (2017): 595–604.

conspiracy mindedness or conspiracy mindedness that causes marginalisation?

Even without definitive answers to these questions, it's interesting that conspiracy mindedness is correlated with negative events. This opens up the possibility that a person's conspiracy mindedness has more to do with that person's life circumstances than with his political ideology. Notice also that these circumstances might include being brought up by conspiracists. Just as one can be a Marxist or a Catholic because one was raised to be one, a person can be a conspiracist because that's how he was raised.

However many objective risk factors for conspiracy mindedness are identified, there is always the possibility that someone who is at risk on all counts doesn't end up as a conspiracist. In the same way, there are conspiracists who display none of the risk factors. What if a person who is well off, white, middle class, and politically moderate still ends up being conspiracy-minded? What explains *his* conspiracism? This question might be difficult to answer, but explaining what makes a person conspiracy-minded isn't just a matter of trying to figure out what pushed him to be like that. There are also pull factors to be taken into account. For all the talk about ideology and negative life events, there's also the fact that Conspiracy Theories are actually *seductive*. If they weren't, they would be totally ineffective as propaganda, so it's worth thinking about their seductiveness. What is it about Conspiracy Theories that hooks people?

One factor is that Conspiracy Theories are *stories*. A good Conspiracy Theory can be just as intriguing and captivating as a good detective novel. The fundamental premise is that the way things really are in the world is quite different from how they seem. White is black and black is white. The Conspiracy Theory consumer is set the challenge of figuring out whodunnit, if not the perpetrators identified by official stories. Who really killed Kennedy, if not Oswald? Who really did 9/11, if not Al Qaeda? When Conspiracy Theories unveil the truth about such events, they have the feel of an Agatha Christie novel identifying the real killer on the last page on the basis of clues that were there all along, if only one had been paying attention.

The analogy with fiction doesn't end there. Conspiracy Theories are morality tales with all-knowing and all-powerful villains and naïve victims who have no idea what is really going on until the truth is revealed by the Conspiracy Theorist. As Rob Brotherton notes, 'the best conspiracy theories have all the trappings of a classic underdog story'.[11] More often than not, the underdog is none other than the brave Conspiracy Theorist, who doggedly takes on the forces of the deep state or the new world order in the interests of making sure that the public knows what's really going on beneath the surface.

Another attraction of Conspiracy Theories is that they invest random events with a deeper significance, which they wouldn't otherwise have. To Princess Diana's many fans, her death in a car accident was so hard to stomach partly because it was so meaningless. How much more comforting to think that it wasn't an accident, that she was the victim of a malicious plot by secret forces! If this is the real story, then she can be regarded as a kind of martyr, just as some Conspiracy Theorists insist on seeing President Kennedy as a martyr.

In a book on religious belief, philosopher Tim Crane argues that the religious impulse can be expressed by the thought that *this can't be all there is; there must be something more to the world*.[12] A similar quasi-religious impulse underpins

---

[11] Brotherton, *Suspicious Minds*, p. 149.
[12] T. Crane, *The Meaning of Belief: Religion from an Atheist's Point of View* (Harvard University Press, 2017), p. 38.

Why Are Conspiracy Theories So Popular?

Conspiracy Theories and accounts for their attractiveness to some people. The impulse in relation to events like the apparently random death of Princess Diana or the killing of President Kennedy by Lee Harvey Oswald is to think that *this can't be all there is to it; there must be something more to these events.*

The idea that Conspiracy Theories give expression to a religious impulse is related to a point I made in chapter 1. In my discussion of the sense in which Conspiracy Theories embody a premodern worldview I said that this comes out in their unwillingness to accept that shit happens, shit like Princess Diana's premature death in a car crash one night in Paris, or the murder of a charismatic young president by a maladjusted no-hoper like Lee Harvey Oswald. The religious impulse is to look for meaning, and one way to satisfy that impulse is to be a Conspiracy Theorist.

All of this might make it seem that Conspiracy Theories are ultimately rather benign, even if they are false. Why knock them if they help some people to cope with the ups and downs of life and politics? Shouldn't they, and the people who believe them, be viewed with sympathy if it's true that Conspiracy Theories are an understandable psychological response to adversity? Up to a point, yes; but it's also important not to forget that the extremist political ideologies that some Conspiracy Theories promote are pretty repugnant. The harm that Conspiracy Theories do needs to be weighed against their very limited benefits.

When it comes to the downside of Conspiracy Theories, the discussion so far has only really scratched the surface. Whatever the consolations of conspiracism or the truth about why some people end up being conspiracy-minded while others do not, the important question is whether Conspiracy Theories are ultimately harmful or beneficial to those who believe them and to society more generally. I'll tackle this question in chapter 3, which is about the actual consequences rather than the causes of conspiracism. These consequences are, or should be, unwelcome.

Meanwhile, the take-home message of this chapter is that there is no simple answer to the question why people are conspiracy-minded. Sometimes it's because of their wider political or ideological commitments. Or it's a response to being marginalised or conspired against. Or it's because Conspiracy Theories satisfy a spiritual need. Or it's some combination of these factors, or something completely different that I haven't mentioned. There is no single or simple explanation of conspiracy mindedness; but there was never any serious hope of that. The answer to the question why people believe Conspiracy Theories is: it's complicated.

3

The Problem with Conspiracy Theories

We live in a world in which governments, including western governments, are often up to no good. They lie, cheat and conspire. There are well-documented examples of conspiracies by US government agencies such as the CIA, and it's vital that their claims about what they are and are not up to are thoroughly investigated. Democracy needs people who are prepared to look into evidence of bad behaviour by our political masters, including evidence of conspiracy. These people are called conspiracy theorists.

This is the thinking that leads philosopher David Coady to conclude that conspiracy theorists are performing an important task on behalf of the community.[1] Coady defines a conspiracy theorist

---

[1] D. Coady, *What to Believe Now: Applying Epistemology to Contemporary Issues* (Wiley Blackwell, 2012).

as a person who is unusually willing to investigate conspiracy. The important social function that conspiracy theorists perform is the function of investigating evidence of political conspiracy. What's more, they serve an important social function even if many of their theories turn out to be incorrect. Even if 9/11 wasn't an inside job, the *possibility* that it was deserves serious consideration. Conspiracy theorists are just the people who give this and other equally worrying possibilities the serious consideration they deserve.

Coady describes the contemporary treatment of those accused of being conspiracy theorists as an intellectual witch hunt. As he sees it, conspiracy theorists are sneered at, condescended to or ignored, in an attempt to intimidate and silence them. Although conspiracy theorists can be *too* willing to believe in conspiracy, Coady argues that they usually only harm themselves. Conspiracy theorists, he suggests, are less harmful than conspiracy sceptics, who are too *unwilling* to believe in conspiracy. These people harm us all by making it easier for conspiracies to remain undetected.

My focus in this book has been on Conspiracy Theorists, people who are excessively willing to believe Conspiracy Theories. These aren't just theories about conspiracies. They are theories about conspiracies that are unlikely to be true for the reasons given in chapter 1. Is it true that Conspiracy Theorists harm only themselves? Imagine being the parent of a child who has just been shot dead at her elementary school and having to listen to people who claim that the shooting was a false flag operation in which no one died. How can anybody think that such theories only harm the people who put them forward?

This chapter is about the various ways in which Conspiracy Theories harm all of us. Coady calls people who vilify conspiracy theories and conspiracy theorists *conspiracy baiters*. He has a problem with conspiracy baiters. My problem is with *conspiracy apologists*, people who make excuses for Conspiracy Theories and downplay the serious harms they do. These are of different kinds: personal, social, intellectual and political. Conspiracy apologists risk becoming apologists for the political causes that Conspiracy Theories have promoted. People who talk about the good that Conspiracy Theories do should think long and hard about this. Our political masters need to be held to account, but spreading wild Conspiracy Theories is the wrong way to do that.

Before looking in more detail at the downside of Conspiracy Theories, it's also worth pointing out that the picture of the Conspiracy Theorists as hapless victims of conspiracy baiters is very hard to recognise. The idea that the modern-day Conspiracy Theorist is capable of being intimidated will certainly amuse anyone who has had the misfortune to debate with one. Conspiracy Theorists aren't the type to be intimidated, and there is little evidence of their being silenced by establishment critics. If you want to know what real intimidation feels like, try writing an article daring to suggest that 9/11 wasn't an inside job. The task of arguing against 9/11 or other Conspiracy Theorists isn't for the faint-hearted or the thin-skinned.

Conspiracy apologists like to say that Conspiracy Theories might be on to something even if they are wrong or too simplistic. Yet the charge sheet against Conspiracy Theories is long and serious. When all the harms they do are weighed against their supposed benefits, there is only one possible verdict: for the most part Conspiracy Theories are not just mistaken but pernicious. Not all theories about conspiracies are pernicious, but Conspiracy Theories are a special case.

The personal harms done by Conspiracy Theories are the harms done to individuals by false accusations of conspiracy. I've already given one example of this. Another illustration of the personal dangers created by Conspiracy Theories is the story of Jim Garrison and Clay Shaw. Garrison was the New Orleans district attorney who charged local businessman Clay Shaw with involvement in a bizarre conspiracy to assassinate President Kennedy. Shaw is still the only person to have been tried for the assassination. Yet there was no credible evidence against him and, when the case went to trial in 1969, it took the jury just forty-five minutes to acquit him. One juror said that it took them that long to acquit Shaw only because several of them had to go to the bathroom. The fact remains, however, that Shaw had to spend his entire life savings on his defence; and the damage to his reputation was irreparable. In his book about the Kennedy assassination, Gerald Posner reports that Shaw died a broken man in 1974.[2]

JFK, Oliver Stone's movie about the Kennedy assassination, portrays Garrison as a hero, yet Posner and others present compelling evidence that he was guilty of bribery, intimidation and abuse of power. Garrison believed that Kennedy had been the victim of a 'homosexual thrill killing' involving up to sixteen assassins, including Shaw.

---

[2] G. Posner, *Case Closed: Lee Harvey Oswald and the Assassination of JFK* (Warner Books, 1993).

What happened to Shaw is an object lesson in how devastating it can be, at a personal level, to be wrongly accused of a major crime by a powerful and ruthless Conspiracy Theorist who believes that black is white and white is black.[3]

Fortunately very few people outside politics will ever be accused of involvement in a major conspiracy; but that's not to say that Conspiracy Theories don't pose a danger to ordinary citizens. When children don't get vaccinated against measles because their parents are taken in by anti-vaccination Conspiracy Theories, they sometimes die. When President Thabo Mbeki delayed the use of antiretrovirals for HIV prevention and treatment in South Africa, thousands of people died unnecessarily from AIDS as a result. Why did Mbeki act as he did? Because he was an AIDS Conspiracy Theorist who believed that the American government was conspiring with drug companies to sell toxic drugs to Africans. When Conspiracy Theories lead to the deaths of thousands of people, we need to give up the idea that these theories are harmless.

---

[3] On Garrison, Shaw and Oliver Stone, see P. Lambert, *False Witness: The Real Story of Jim Garrison's Investigation and Oliver Stone's Film JFK* (M. Evans & Company, 1998).

The Problem with Conspiracy Theories

Causing unnecessary deaths is an example of a serious social harm. The social harms caused by Conspiracy Theories are related to the ways in which they are *intellectually* harmful. One such way is the fact that they prevent us from knowing things that we would otherwise know. Conspiracy Theories are obstacles to knowledge and, because of that, they are also harmful to us in other ways.

For example, imagine a parent who is advised by his doctor to give his child the MMR vaccine (i.e. the vaccine against measles, mumps and rubella). Suppose that the doctor bases her advice on well-conducted research showing that the vaccine is safe and effective. Assuming that the doctor is trustworthy, the parent is now in a position to *know* that the vaccine is safe and effective. Philosophers describe this type of knowledge as *testimonial* knowledge: knowing by being told by someone who already knows.

Now imagine that the same parent decides to do his own research and comes across anti-vaxxer websites alleging that the MMR vaccine causes autism in children. In fact research claiming a link between the MMR vaccine and autism has been totally discredited, but the parent isn't aware of that. As a result of his encounter with anti-vaxxer Conspiracy Theories, he now has no confidence that the vaccine is safe. The point at which he starts to doubt the safety of the vaccine is the point at which he no longer knows that the vaccine is safe. He has gone from knowing something (that the vaccine is safe) to not knowing, but *not because of any change in the facts*. His loss of knowledge is due to the doubts implanted in his mind by anti-vaxxer Conspiracy Theories.

In general, for us to know that something is the case, that thing actually has to *be* the case. You can't know that the MMR vaccine is safe if it isn't. You can't know that 9/11 was an inside job if it wasn't. In addition, to know that something is the case, you have to be confident that it is the case. You don't know that the vaccine is safe unless you are confident that it is safe. Not absolutely certain but at least reasonably confident; you must at least *believe* that the vaccine is safe in order to know that it is safe. But even that isn't enough for knowledge, if it turns out that your confidence is misplaced. It matters whether you have the right to be confident. So you know that the vaccine is safe only if (i) it is safe, (ii) you are confident that it is safe, and (iii) you have the *right* to be confident.

In my example, the parent has the right to be confident that the vaccine is safe but isn't actually confident. He has the right to be confident because a trustworthy source – his doctor – has told him that it's safe. He isn't actually confident because of the psychological impact of anti-vaxxer propaganda. Websites that question the 'official' view of the MMR vaccine leave people like my imaginary parent in the position of not knowing what to think. Not knowing what to think about whether the vaccine is safe amounts to not knowing whether the vaccine is safe. It amounts, in other words, to a form of ignorance or being in the dark.

Anti-vaxxer Conspiracy Theorists will insist that there is no loss of knowledge in my example because the parent never knew that the vaccine is safe to begin with. How could he have known this, if the vaccine isn't safe? He never *had* the right to be confident in the safety of the vaccine, and hence didn't *lose* the right. If he is no longer confident that the vaccine is safe, then, as far as the anti-vaxxer is concerned, that is exactly how things should be.

But why should the confused parent have any confidence in what the anti-vaxxer says about the safety of the vaccine? Would he have the right to be confident that the vaccine causes autism in children, given that the medical establishment, as represented by his doctor, has assured him that it doesn't? It all depends on what is involved in having the right to be confident. In general, if somebody tells you that something is so, what does it take for you to have the right to be confident that it is so?

For a start, your source must be *qualified* and *trustworthy*. One way to be qualified is to be an expert. We all rely on experts to know much of what we know. I know that my heart is in good shape because my cardiologist told me so. I know that my car needs a new battery because a qualified car mechanic told me that it does. A qualified mechanic might tell me that my car needs a new battery even if it doesn't, and that's where trustworthiness comes in. In order for me to know, on the basis of what the mechanic tells me, that my car needs a new battery, he actually needs to be trustworthy and I actually need to trust him. Without trust and trustworthiness there is no testimonial knowledge.

Being qualified is often a matter of having actual qualifications, obtained by study. The cardiologist who tells me about my heart has degrees to prove that she is an expert. Another aspect of being qualified is having the right kind of experience. An experienced cardiologist is more qualified to tell me about my heart than someone fresh out of medical school. Lastly, a genuine expert is one who is recognised as an expert by her peers. If nobody else in her profession thinks she is any good, then she isn't an expert.

The Problem with Conspiracy Theories

By this standard, very few Conspiracy Theorists are experts in the technical subjects that their theories depend on. This goes back to what I was saying in chapter 1 about the sheer amateurishness of Conspiracy Theories. Few Conspiracy Theorists about the assassination of President Kennedy have any expertise in forensics or wound ballistics. Few 9/11 Conspiracy Theorists have any expertise in civil engineering or building construction. And many anti-vaxxers have no medical qualifications whatsoever. So how can anybody have the right to be confident in their theories?

Conspiracy Theorists will say that, although many of them aren't qualified, they rely for their theories on people who are. But that's very often not the case. Consider the debate about the safety of the MMR vaccine. It's true that back in 1998 Dr Andrew Wakefield published a paper in a respectable medical journal speculating that the MMR vaccine might cause autism in children. Wakefield had medical qualifications and experience. But the paper was retracted in 2010 and Wakefield lost his licence to practise medicine in the United Kingdom after being found guilty by the General Medical Council of dishonesty and ethics violations. In no sense is he recognised by the majority of his peers as an expert concerning the link between the MMR vaccine and autism. So his work provides anti-vaxxer Conspiracy Theorists with no right to be confident that the vaccine is unsafe.

Faced with the discrediting of their 'experts', Conspiracy Theorists do one of two things. One is to suggest that, just because their experts aren't recognised as such by their establishment peers, it doesn't mean that they aren't experts. Who is and isn't a real expert is all relative to one's point of view, so anti-vaxxers are perfectly entitled to regard Wakefield as an expert by their own lights. The other response is to say that there is something wrong with the whole idea of expertise and deferring to experts. This was the view that the British politician Michael Gove was expressing when he famously claimed, during the Brexit debate in the United Kingdom, that 'the people of this country have had enough of experts'.[4] The implication was that to regard the opinions of experts as having greater validity than the opinions of non-experts is a form of elitism that 'the people of this country' reject.

Either response is a form of intellectual suicide. Given how much there is to know and how little

---

[4] See the report, in the *Financial Times*, of Gove's 2016 interview with Faisal Islam of Sky News: https://www.ft.com/content/3be49734-29cb-11e6-83e4-abc22d5d108c.

even the cleverest and most educated human being will ever know, we all have to rely on experts. If we rely on experts to know the condition of our hearts or cars, it is absurd to think that we shouldn't rely on experts to know the economic impact of Brexit or the safety of vaccines. What is more, it isn't a matter of opinion who is and who isn't an expert. There are objective measures of expertise, and an expert isn't just someone whose views are the same as mine. Saying that is just another way of dismissing the whole idea of genuine expertise.

When Conspiracy Theorists attack experts who disagree with them or proclaim that they have had enough of experts, they are contributing to what author Tom Nichols calls 'the death of expertise'.[5] The death of expertise isn't the death of *actual* expertise, that is, of the special abilities and knowledge that some people have. Rather it is what Nichols describes as 'a rejection of science and dispassionate rationality'.[6] When study after study fails to establish a link between MMR and autism, it is a rejection of science and dispassionate

[5] T. Nichols, *The Death of Expertise: The Campaign against Established Knowledge and Why It Matters* (Oxford University Press, 2017).
[6] Ibid., p. 5.

rationality to insist that there is a link. When experts – that is, *genuine* experts – say that it was possible for aircraft impacts to bring down the twin towers on 9/11, it is a rejection of science and dispassionate rationality to go on insisting that it wasn't possible. It makes no difference that a handful of experts in fields other than building safety and civil engineering have a different view. They aren't competent to judge.

Contributing to the death of expertise is not just intellectually harmful in its own right; it also explains how Conspiracy Theories are obstacles to knowledge. Given how much we all rely on experts to know about the world we live in, anything that prevents us from acquiring knowledge from experts is an obstacle to knowledge more generally. It's difficult to imagine anything that more effectively prevents us from acquiring knowledge from experts than the suggestion that there is no good reason to rely on them, or the notion that who is and isn't an expert is a purely subjective matter. It isn't.

What about Conspiracy Theorists who aren't anti-expert and don't think that expertise is a subjective matter? Why couldn't there be such theorists? The problem is that in most of the areas in which Conspiracy Theorists operate actual expert opinion is against them. That's true of vaccine safety, civil engineering, Nazi history and just about every other specialist discipline that is relevant to the most prominent Conspiracy Theories. That's why amateur Conspiracy Theorists can't avoid being anti-expert. They would have to give up their theories if they were serious about not being anti-expert. As it is, the only experts whose opinions they want to hear are other Conspiracy Theorists.

By contributing to the death of expertise, Conspiracy Theories are also accountable for some of the political consequences of anti-expertise. In any case, the intellectual and the political can't always be neatly separated. Conspiracies Theories helped to create the intellectual and political climate that resulted in Brexit in the United Kingdom and in the election of Donald Trump, himself something of a Conspiracy Theorist, as US president.

It's no surprise that Conspiracy Theories have political consequences. If their role is to promote a political cause, then Conspiracy Theories are as politically harmful as the causes they promote. A number of these causes have been extremist, racist causes. Although Conspiracy Theorists might dissociate themselves from such causes, it is nevertheless true, as Byford notes, that they operate in an ideological space with a long anti-Semitic tradition. That ideological space is one that has been occupied by fascists and other extremists, and this is an inescapable fact that any analysis of what Conspiracy Theories mean in practice has to acknowledge.

Conspiracy Theorists who aren't right-wing extremists may well think that all this talk of an anti-Semitic tradition of Conspiracy Theories is a blatantly unfair attempt to discredit them by association. After all, why should the anti-Semitism of some notorious Conspiracy Theories be held against Conspiracy Theorists who explicitly disso-ciate themselves from fascism and anti-Semitism? Why should politically moderate Conspiracy Theorists carry the can for the sins of their extremist brethren?

This is a fair enough question and the answer to it is complicated. For a start, there is the issue of what it is to dissociate oneself from anti-Semitism. It's easy to say that one's theory doesn't target a particular group, while making it clear in other ways that it does. As Michael Billig points out, 'the perpetual stress on Jewish names in conspiracy publications serves to create the impression that all the hated conspirators are Jews'.[7] This kind of

---

[7] M. Billig, *Fascists: A Social Psychological View of the National Front* (Harcourt Brace Jovanovich, 1978), p. 299.

implicit scapegoating is far from unusual in the world of Conspiracy Theories. In many ways it is more pernicious than the outright racism of overtly anti-Semitic theories.

A deeper problem for moderate Conspiracy Theorists is that the meaning and ultimate political significance of Conspiracy Theories is something over which they have no control. There is no getting around the fact that Conspiracy Theories are part of a predominantly, though not exclusively, right-wing political tradition. While it might seem unfair to condemn non-racist Conspiracy Theorists for the sins of racist Conspiracy Theorists, the issue of guilt by association is much more complicated than it seems. There is a sense in which, by endorsing Conspiracy Theories, one can't help associating oneself with the political causes that these theories have traditionally promoted. Whether or not individual Conspiracy Theorists realise it, their theories come with political baggage.

Think of this analogy: the Confederate flag is a symbol of the American South, with its history of slavery and racial oppression. In recent years the flag has been adopted as a symbol by white suprem-acists such as Dylann Roof, who in 2015 murdered nine African Americans at a church in Charleston, South Carolina. Many public institutions in the southern United States no longer display the flag, and its use remains controversial. Now imagine a white southerner who chooses to display the flag in her porch but claims that it is just an expression of pride in her southern heritage. In her mind, racism and slavery have nothing to do with it.

But what the flag actually symbolises isn't determined by the beliefs and intentions of the individual who chooses to display it. The flag has a life of its own, its own history and meaning, and doesn't become politically benign just because the person displaying it doesn't think of it as a symbol of slavery and racism. Its history is its history and its meaning is its meaning. People who display the flag are, wittingly or unwittingly, associating themselves with what it *in fact* symbolises, regardless of their personal views. They are guilty by association and have no grounds for complaint if their African American neighbours are offended by the sight of the flag on their houses or cars.

In the same way, Conspiracy Theories have a life of their own, with their own history and meaning. They symbolise a particular worldview, and that worldview is one that has always scapegoated and demonised particular groups of people – Jewish people more often than not. The non-racist who insists that Conspiracy Theories per se have got nothing to do with anti-Semitism is in the same position as the southerner who argues that the Confederate flag per se has nothing to do with slavery. In both cases the answer is the same: *you don't get to decide what things mean.* The history of Conspiracy Theories is not something from which even politically progressive Conspiracy Theorists can separate themselves.

This helps to explain an interesting political phenomenon described by Chip Berlet: the use of Conspiracy Theories by people on the political right to woo people on the political left.[8] Berlet notes that the flourishing of far-right ideologies in the United States has created a dynamic whereby people from far-right groups try to make common cause with left-wing activists over issues of common concern, such as opposition to US involvement in the Middle East. Conspiracy Theories are a highly effective tool for forging such alliances, given their popularity at both ends of the political spectrum.

The blurring of the line between left and right in the world of Conspiracy Theories should be a problem for conspiracy apologists who are at the progressive rather than at the conservative end of

---

[8] C. Berlet's *Right Woos Left*, at https://www.politicalresearch. org/1999/02/27/right-woos-left.

the political spectrum. Conspiracy apologists think that people who attack Conspiracy Theories must be friends or agents of the western political establishment. For example, if a Conspiracy Theory blames the Bush administration for 9/11, then doesn't it follow that people who say that this theory is hogwash must be friends of the Bush administration? But the fact that a person criticises Conspiracy Theories doesn't mean that this person can't be as critical of governments and government agencies.

The relevance of this can be illustrated by looking at the views of Charles Pigden, a philosopher who has made a name for himself as a conspiracy apologist.[9] He targets the principle that, in general, we shouldn't believe conspiracy theories. He argues that this principle is plainly absurd, since people often conspire. If people often conspire, then there is nothing wrong with believing that they do. More to the point here, the principle that we shouldn't believe conspiracy theories also helps conspiracy-prone western political leaders to get away with murder.

---

[9] C. Pigden, 'Conspiracy theories and the conventional wisdom', *Episteme: A Journal of Social Epistemology* 4 (2007): 219–32.

The Problem with Conspiracy Theories

According to Pigden, when people say we shouldn't believe conspiracy theories, what they really mean is that we shouldn't believe conspiracy theories that accuse *western* governments of involvement in evil schemes. Yet we now know that the Kennedy administration conspired to overthrow the Diem government in Vietnam, that the Nixon administration was up to its eyeballs in the Watergate conspiracy, and that the Reagan administration conspired to sell weapons to Iran in order to fund the Contras in Nicaragua. Given these and many other cases of conspiratorial behaviour by western governments, can it possibly make sense to make it a rule to dismiss theories that accuse them of wrongdoing?

Nobody in their right mind would recommend such a policy, and certainly not people whose objection to Conspiracy Theories is that they promote right-wing causes. Anyway, as we saw in chapter 1, a Conspiracy Theory isn't simply a theory that posits a conspiracy. It's a theory about a conspiracy that is unlikely to be true. Not believing such theories is quite consistent with believing evidence-based historical accounts of actual conspiracies, including accounts of conspiracies mounted by western governments. The problem with Conspiracy Theories is not that they accuse western governments of conspiracy but that they aren't based on solid evidence and have a political agenda that conspiracy apologists should look at long and hard before leaping to their defence.

In general, conspiracy apologists have surprisingly little to say about the actual history of Conspiracy Theories or about the political causes they have been used to promote. The anti-Semitism of many Conspiracy Theories is either not mentioned at all or only mentioned in passing. But if Conspiracy Theories are used to promote right-wing anti-Semitic causes, then conspiracy apologists and Conspiracy Theorists make strange bedfellows. The enemy of my enemy is not necessarily my friend. The fact that Conspiracy Theorists and conspiracy apologists share a strong dislike for western foreign policy isn't an excuse for conspiracy apologists to overlook the history and political associations of Conspiracy Theories.

To see the difference between being a critic of western governments and being a Conspiracy Theorist, you only need to look at Noam Chomsky. It's hard to imagine a more passionate or more ardent critic of successive American and other western governments. Yet Chomsky is no Conspiracy Theorist. When asked about 9/11 Conspiracy Theories, he pointed out that the Bush administration would have had to be utterly insane to try anything like what is alleged by the 9/11 Truth movement. In his view, there is no credible evidence that 9/11 was an inside job or a false flag operation. However, his main objection to Conspiracy Theories is that they are a distraction from more serious matters.[10]

What could be more serious than a government conspiracy that results in the destruction of the twin towers and the death of three thousand civilians? Many Conspiracy Theorists think that 9/11 was an inside job because they think it gave President Bush an excuse to invade Iraq. 9/11 and the 2003 invasion of Iraq are closely connected in many people's minds, and this makes it all too easy for opposition to Bush's Iraq policy to morph into support for 9/11 Conspiracy Theories. Indeed, Conspiracy Theories about 9/11 became, at least for a while, a popular way to express opposition to US involvement in Iraq. Conspiracy apologists who don't believe that 9/11 was an inside job may have a more sympathetic view of people who think that it was, because they share their strong disapproval of the foreign policy that led to the invasion.

---

[10] Visit https://zcomm.org/zblogs/9-11-institutional-analysis-vs-conspiracy-theory-by-noam-chomsky.

The Problem with Conspiracy Theories

But, if you are against US policy in Iraq, then why not just criticise that policy directly? Why muddy the waters by adding that 9/11 was an inside job? Criticising the Bush administration on that basis only diminishes the credibility of criticisms of its failed Iraq policy, and that's one sense in which Conspiracy Theories are not just a distraction but counterproductive. Indeed, if one were being really cynical, one might think that, in a strange way, 9/11 Conspiracy Theories were *good* for the Bush administration, because they made it easier for it to portray its critics as unhinged.

Aside from their impact on our understanding of historical events like 9/11 or the invasion of Iraq, Conspiracy Theories are also a distraction from big-picture social issues such as injustice and inequality. For example, there is evidence that the already substantial gap between rich and poor in many countries, including the United States, is widening. Not everyone cares about that, or for that matter about gender inequality, racial oppression and countless other serious social issues. However, Conspiracy Theorists and conspiracy apologists who do care should ask themselves whether it might not be a better use of their time to focus on these issues rather than on the plausibility or otherwise of arcane theories about 9/11 or the assassination of a president more than half a century ago.

When it comes to big-picture social developments, there isn't much temptation to suppose that conspiracies are to blame. Conspiratorial explanations are personal; they explain significant events by talking about the secret decisions, plans and activities of small groups of people. The contrast is with *institutional* or *structural* explanations, which are much more impersonal. For example, growing inequality can be explained by the structure and institutions of capitalist economies. It isn't the product of individual decision-making.

One effect of obsessing about events that are best explained in personal rather than structural terms is to divert attention away from social issues that are best explained in structural rather than personal terms. If the causes of society's deepest problems are institutional or structural, then the solution is institutional or structural. Conspiracy Theorists and apologists like to think of themselves as serious critics of the status quo, yet their activities divert public attention away from the deeper structural issues that ought to concern any serious critic. From this perspective, the questions to which Conspiracy Theories claim to provide answers are the wrong questions.

Despite this, could it not still be argued that Conspiracy Theorists perform an important task on behalf of the community? I started this chapter by discussing David Coady's approach to conspiracy theories. His defence of these theories and of the people who support them is simple and at least superficially appealing: we live in a world in which conspiracies take place on a regular basis. Because political conspiracies are common and it's a good thing that they are exposed, it is important that there are people who are willing to investigate evidence of political conspiracy. If it's a good thing that conspiracies are exposed, then it's a good thing that there are people who are willing to expose them.

The problem with this is that in the real world Conspiracy Theorists tend not to be serious and impartial seekers of truth who base their claims of conspiracy on actual evidence of conspiracy. That's what makes them Conspiracy Theories with a capital C and a capital T. They are often more like Jim Garrison in that they are too willing to believe in conspiracy. They exaggerate evidence of conspiracy and ignore evidence against their theories.

What the community needs, if it is to look into evidence of political conspiracy, is people with sound judgement, relevant expertise and good investigative skills. People with these attributes are unlikely to be Conspiracy Theorists, with their strange obsessions and habit of jumping to sensational conclusions on the basis of flimsy or non-existent evidence. Conspiracy Theorists are above all propagandists. They pretend to be serious researchers but the reality is that their theories tend to be politics-based rather than evidence-based. They might occasionally get something right, but that is more a matter of luck than of judgement. A nation that actually wants to know the truth about 9/11 shouldn't be relying on the insights of a bunch of right-wing talk-show hosts and retired academics.

It's not that conspiracy apologists are unaware of the gap between the theory and the reality of Conspiracy Theories. The problem is that they underestimate the extent of the gap and idealise Conspiracy Theorists. The ideal theorist is unbiased, analyses evidence of conspiracy in a calm and reasonable manner, and doesn't imagine that spending a few hours on the Internet makes her an expert in forensic science, civil engineering or other technical subjects relevant to her theories. The question one has to ask is: how many actual Conspiracy Theorists are like this? Frothing at the mouth and ranting about the evils of the deep state or of the Jews is not what one wants from one's Conspiracy Theorists. All too often it is what one gets.

Where does all of this leave the suggestion I mentioned at the start of this chapter, that being too willing to believe in conspiracy is less harmful than being too unwilling? Suppose it's true that being reluctant to believe in conspiracy raises the chances that some genuine conspiracies will go undetected. That is, no doubt, a bad thing; but is it worse than peddling theories that result in thousands of people dying of AIDS, or in the decline of public trust in genuine experts? It's hard to measure these things or weigh one kind of harm against another, but on the face of it the idea that being a Conspiracy Theory sceptic is worse than being a Conspiracy Theorist doesn't have a lot going for it.

It's also worth thinking about *why* people are unwilling to believe in conspiracy. Sometimes this attitude is the result of a kind of a pro-establishment bias, but there is also the embarrassment factor: the behaviour and political affiliations of prominent Conspiracy Theorists make it embarrassing to be thought of as being one of them. The only people who are to blame for that are the Conspiracy Theorists themselves. By lowering the tone of political debate, they give the impression that a

The Problem with Conspiracy Theories

Conspiracy Theorist is not a respectable thing to be. As a result, and perhaps paradoxically, Conspiracy Theorists have actually made it more likely that genuine conspiracies will remain undetected. If you want people to take you seriously, don't be a jerk.

All of this leaves us facing a practical problem. If Conspiracy Theories are really as problematic as I've been arguing, then what should we do about them? Should we try to rebut them or is it better to ignore them, since nothing is going to change the Conspiracy Theorist's mind anyway? That sounds tempting, especially given how bruising arguments with Conspiracy Theorists can be. At the same time, how can it be right to leave Conspiracy Theories unchallenged, if they are harmful in the ways that I have been describing? These are the questions I'll be tackling in the final chapter of this book.

4

How to Respond to Conspiracy Theories

Speaking to the *Washington Post* in 2004, Philip Zelikow, the executive director of the official 9/11 Commission, explained the Commission's attitude towards 9/11 conspiracy theories. 'We discussed the theories', Zelikow told the *Post*, but 'when we wrote the report, we were also careful not to answer all the theories. It's like playing Whack-A-Mole. You're never going to whack them all. ... What we tried to do instead was to affirmatively tell what was true and tell it adding a lot of critical details that we knew would help dispel concerns.'[1]

If 'whacking' a Conspiracy Theory is the same as rebutting it – proving that it's false – then the Commission was in an even tougher position than Zelikow describes. It's not just that there are too

---

[1] Quoted in the *Washington Post*, 7 October 2004.

many Conspiracy Theories to keep up with and rebut. The problem is that rebutting a theory won't necessarily persuade its supporters to give it up. Rebutting is one thing, persuading is another; it is *theories* that are rebutted (or not), but *people* who are persuaded (or not). Whether a theory has been rebutted depends on whether it has *in fact* been proved to be false using good arguments and trustworthy information. Persuasion also requires that the person you are trying to persuade *accepts* that his theory has been disproved. Experience suggests that Conspiracy Theorists tend not to be persuaded by arguments against their theories. There aren't too many examples of committed Conspiracy Theorists changing their minds.

If one doesn't have the patience to play whack-a-mole – and one probably isn't going to get anywhere with Conspiracy Theorists even if one does – then it seems that the only alternative is to ignore them. Why waste precious time and energy trying to persuade the unpersuadable? Apart from anything else, there is a danger that engaging with Conspiracy Theorists to the extent of actually arguing with them only serves to draw attention to their views and gives the impression that they are at least worth discussing.

But ignoring Conspiracy Theories isn't satisfactory either. If they are harmful, then surely

they shouldn't be allowed to proliferate unchallenged. There's also something deeply arrogant
about judging that theories that millions of people
believe aren't even worthy of *consideration*. No
doubt there are some Conspiracy Theories that are
too outlandish to bother with, but can it really be
said that this is true of all Conspiracy Theories?
For example, don't Conspiracy Theories about 9/11
deserve at least a response? But this takes us back
to the whack-a-mole problem and the apparent
futility of trying to change the minds of Conspiracy
Theorists.

These are some of the issues tackled by Cass
Sunstein and Adrian Vermeule in a famous article
that succeeded in enraging many Conspiracy
Theorists.[2] One of their more notorious proposals
is that governments should respond to hard-core
conspiracy theories by engaging in what they call
cognitive infiltration. By this they don't mean spying.
Their idea is that government agents, acting either
anonymously or openly, should enter Internet chat
rooms, social networks or real-space groups and
try to 'undermine percolating conspiracy theories
by raising doubts about their factual premises,

---

[2] C. Sunstein and A. Vermeule, 'Conspiracy theories: Causes
and cures', *Journal of Political Philosophy* 17 (2009): 202–27.

causal logic, or implications for action, political or otherwise'.[3]

This seems a good idea to Sunstein and Vermeule because of their account of how conspiracy theories arise and spread. They think that conspiracy theorists end up believing the things they believe because they suffer from a 'crippled epistemology'. In other words, people end up believing Conspiracy Theories not because they are irrational but because they have little relevant information and their views are supported by what little they know.

The idea that a Conspiracy Theorist who lives in the West with full Internet access lacks relevant information about events such as 9/11 seems a little odd. The problem for most people in that situation is not that they have too little information but that they have too much. But, however much information we have at our fingertips, we don't regard all information as equal. We look to some sources of information rather than others and are more or less inclined to believe what we are told depending on who is doing the telling and whether it is in line with what we already think. Confirmation bias means that we seek out information that confirms our preexisting views while avoiding or ignoring contrary views.

---

[3] Ibid., pp. 224–5.

The result is the creation of self-sustaining belief bubbles from which other voices have been filtered out. People in the same belief bubble share the same basic assumptions and opinions. They reinforce each other's opinions and don't allow their basic assumptions to be questioned. Anyone who questions their assumptions is excluded from the bubble, for example by being 'unfriended' on Facebook or 'unfollowed' on Twitter. It isn't just Conspiracy Theorists who do this. We all enjoy the comfort of inhabiting belief bubbles and we are all subject to confirmation bias.

The belief bubble that Conspiracy Theorists inhabit is one that rejects officially sanctioned experts or sources of information. They have their own sources of information – conspiracy websites, for example – and their own experts. If they suffer from a crippled epistemology, it isn't because they lack information but because their 'information' isn't reliable and their 'experts' aren't really experts. In the world of Conspiracy Theories, David Ray Griffin is authoritative about 9/11, the 9/11 Commission is not; anti-vaxxer websites are regarded as trusted sources of information about the MMR vaccine, the World Health Organisation is not. Indeed, if one is a Conspiracy Theorist, then one is likely to view official attempts to question one's theories as part of a cover-up, part of the very conspiracy one is trying to uncover.

This partly accounts for what Sunstein and Vermeule call the *self-sealing* quality of Conspiracy Theories: the arguments that give rise to them and account for their plausibility make it more difficult for outsiders to challenge them. 'They would say that, wouldn't they?' is the Conspiracy Theorist's stock response to government officials who dispute their theories. Contrary evidence is dismissed either as 'fake news' or as part of the conspiracy. It's hard to win an argument with a person whose fundamental assumptions and ways of thinking are completely different from yours.

I said in chapter 1 that Conspiracy Theories have a number of special features that distinguish them from more mundane theories about conspiracies: they are speculative, contrarian, esoteric, amateurish and premodern. To this list it's now necessary to add another feature: Conspiracy Theories are self-sealing. But, if that's right, then it's difficult to see how cognitive infiltration can be an effective response, if an effective response is defined as one that actually persuades whomever one is trying to persuade.

Take the premise that it was physically impossible for aircraft impacts and the resulting fires to have brought down the twin towers on 9/11. That's a premise that is widely believed in the 9/11 Conspiracy Theory belief bubble. Now imagine a government agent infiltrating the bubble and raising doubts about its validity. The self-sealing quality of Conspiracy Theories means that such doubts will probably be not just rejected but ridiculed. Rather than changing minds, cognitive infiltration will almost certainly result in the infiltrator being ostracised and ejected from the bubble. Being unmasked as a government agent or confessing to being one will further reduce this person's chances of being taken seriously.

Apart from the self-sealing nature of Conspiracy Theories, another obstacle to effective cognitive infiltration is the so-called 'backfire effect'. Studies by social psychologists have looked into how easily false or unsubstantiated political beliefs can be corrected. In one well-known study subjects were given mock news articles that included both a misleading claim by a politician and a correction. For example, they were first shown news reports of President Bush claiming that Iraq has weapons of mass destruction (WMD) and then news reports of a study showing that in fact Iraq didn't have WMD.[4]

---

[4] B. Nyhan and J. Reifler, 'When corrections fail', *Political Behavior* 32 (2010): 303–30.

How to Respond to Conspiracy Theories

Did people who believed the initial report give up the belief that Iraq had WMD after reading the correction? They did not. The correction either had no effect or in some cases *strengthened* the impression that Iraq had WMD. This is the backfire effect, where corrections increase misperceptions. Furthermore, ideology makes a significant difference to how people respond to corrections. Where the initial story is in line with the subject's preexisting political or ideological convictions, the correction is more likely to produce a backfire effect.

The backfire effect looks like a serious problem for attempts to change minds by cognitive infiltration. In the case of an ideologically committed 9/11 Truther who believes that aircraft impacts couldn't have brought down the twin towers, what are the likely consequences if a government agent who has infiltrated the Truther's belief bubble raises doubts about this belief? It now looks as though the result might actually be to *strengthen* the Truther's belief. The more politically committed the Conspiracy Theorist, the more likely it is that the correction will produce a backfire effect. Given that Conspiracy Theories are, by and large, an expression of a person's ideology, there is no getting around this.

The underlying problem is that challenging a Conspiracy Theory isn't a matter of challenging a set of beliefs that the believer can easily give up when presented with contrary evidence. Beliefs such as the one about whether aircraft impacts could have brought down the twin towers are ones to which many Conspiracy Theorists are personally committed at a very deep level. Conspiracy Theories aren't just theories. They are expressions of a particular view about how the world works, and can't be shaken without changing the Conspiracy Theorists' overall worldview. That is just not something that can be done by quoting official studies and experts. A person with the Conspiracy Theorist's worldview is obviously going to see these studies and experts as tainted.

So where do we go from here? On the one hand, Conspiracy Theories are too important and corrosive to ignore. On the other hand, rebutting a Conspiracy Theory is unlikely to change the minds of people who are passionately committed to it and might even end up having the opposite effect. The way forward is just to accept from the outset that there is a hard core of Conspiracy Theorists who aren't going to change their minds whatever one says. Especially in cases where there is a clear financial or ideological motive for promoting a particular theory, it's not going to help to point out that the theory has been rebutted. The rebuttal won't be seen as effective and, in any case, there may be conspiracy entrepreneurs who don't really believe their own theories.

A more promising and worthwhile target of rebuttal efforts is people with a weaker commitment to Conspiracy Theories, or the presumably large numbers of those who are curious about such theories, maybe even receptive to them, without yet being true believers. This is where there is some hope of getting somewhere. What is needed is a strategy that has a realistic chance of dissuading the undecided or moderate Conspiracy Theorists from fully going over to the dark side. The most seductive and serious Conspiracy Theories are politically motivated, but also have some semblance of intellectual respectability. An effective strategy for countering the spread of such theories will need to have both an intellectual and a political dimension.

Starting with the intellectual dimension, it's no good rejecting Conspiracy Theories unless one has solid intellectual grounds for doing so. Maybe there are some Conspiracy Theories – the theory that planet Earth is under the control of shape-shifting reptilians is one example – whose inherent absurdity means that no further argument is needed. Some 'theories' are too silly to need refuting by argument. But many Conspiracy Theories aren't like that. In the case of Conspiracy Theories that have recognisably intellectual foundations, the first step in dealing with them is to undermine those foundations.

In many cases this is no easy task, because of the specialist knowledge required to do the undermining and the sheer number of theories to contend with. But, even if one doesn't want to play whack-a-mole with Conspiracy Theories, it's worth pointing out that many theories about the same event share a core set of basic assumptions. For example, in the case of the Kennedy assassination, many Conspiracy Theories share the assumption that a single bullet couldn't have caused the injuries to Kennedy and Governor Connally. By identifying and rebutting this core assumption one might hope to knock out a whole bunch of assassination Conspiracy Theories in one go.

A model for how to do this is Gerald Posner's book on the Kennedy assassination, *Case Closed*. Over the course of five hundred pages Posner carefully, patiently and systematically dismantles every major Conspiracy Theory about the assassination. He gives a compelling account of how a single bullet could have injured the president and the governor and, in the process, corrects other common misconceptions among Conspiracy

Theorists. He effectively challenges the view that the truth about the assassination is unknowable and shows that 'the troubling issues and questions about the assassination can be settled, the issue of who killed JFK resolved, and Oswald's motivation revealed'.[5]

Of course, hard-core Conspiracy Theorists aren't going to be persuaded by Posner's *tour de force*. For them there is no question of the case being closed, and the backfire effect might mean that their conviction that Oswald didn't act alone is strengthened rather than weakened by Posner's painstaking arguments. But, for less committed Conspiracy Theorists or for people with open minds about the assassination, having the case against Conspiracy Theories about the assassination laid out in such detail might do some good.

More accurately, Posner's arguments might convince impartial readers who have the time and interest to read a dense five hundred-page book about the assassination. The worry is that only dedicated conspiracy buffs will read Posner; but dedicated conspiracy buffs are the hardest to convince. When it comes to Conspiracy Theories the

[5] G. Posner, *Case Closed: Lee Harvey Oswald and the Assassination of JFK* (Warner Books, 1993), p. xi.

problem isn't that there isn't compelling evidence against them. The problem is that the compelling evidence against them is often buried in books and reports that may be too scholarly for many readers.

Another illustration of this difficulty is the phenomenon of Holocaust denial. The historian David Irving has for many years promoted the idea that Hitler didn't order the extermination of the Jews in Europe. In support of this claim he quotes a phone log of a conversation between two senior Nazis in 1941 concerning an order supposedly given by Hitler to the effect that there was to be no liquidation of the Jews. For non-specialists it can be hard to rebut such claims, and this might account for the growth of Conspiracy Theories about the Holocaust.

The fact is, though, that Irving's claim about Hitler's order *has* been refuted by the Cambridge historian Richard J. Evans.[6] As Evans clearly shows, Irving mistranslates and misrepresents the phone log. Hitler's instruction concerned *one* transport of Jews from Berlin. The log didn't contain a general order from Hitler or anyone else to stop the killing of Jews. But how many people have the time or inclination to delve into scholarly debates about

---

[6] See Richard J. Evans, *Lying about Hitler: History, Holocaust and the David Irving Trial* (Basic Books, 2002).

the correct translation of a phone log from 1941, or to read a book like Evans's? It's not that Evans doesn't write well, but reading serious books is a minority pastime.

The only way around this is for people who have taken the trouble to find out the facts to use all means at their disposal, from social media to private conversations, to publicise these facts and to challenge unfounded Conspiracy Theories. When faced with theories that distort the facts, the motto should be: rebut, rebut, rebut.[7] The aim should always be to tell the truth. While this might have little effect on committed Conspiracy Theorists, these aren't the people one should be trying to convince. The aim should be to prevent the spread of Conspiracy Theories by equipping as many people as possible with the resources that can help them to see for themselves what is wrong with such theories.

Bringing out the ways in which Conspiracy Theories are intellectually flawed is one way to discredit them, but it is not the only way. There is also the political dimension of an effective response

---

[7] As I argue in my TEDx talk 'Conspiracy theories and the problem of disappearing knowledge', at https://www.youtube.com/watch?v=h-eQ2bR1HFk.

to Conspiracy Theories. A political response to Conspiracy Theories will need to do at least three things: make the case that many Conspiracy Theories are forms of political propaganda rather than serious attempts to tell the truth; show that one can criticise Conspiracy Theories without being an apologist for government misconduct; and be careful to respect the distinction between Conspiracy Theories and conspiracy theories. In addition, obviously enough, there is one thing that an effective political response to Conspiracy Theories should definitely *refrain* from doing – namely promoting and spreading a different set of Conspiracy Theories.

I've already defended the propaganda model of Conspiracy Theories, the view that many of these theories are forms of political propaganda. If I'm right about this, then it's important that no opportunity is missed to point out the role of Conspiracy Theories as propaganda. If their function is to advance a political agenda, then that fact needs to be highlighted. Here are the questions one should insist on coming back to. What is it that people who promote Conspiracy Theories are trying to achieve, and what do they have to gain, politically or in other ways, from their theories being taken up? What is their ideological agenda? *Cui bono*?

How to Respond to Conspiracy Theories

This approach is especially worthwhile with left-leaning Conspiracy Theory consumers. As I've noted, left-leaning critics of the 2003 US invasion of Iraq may find Conspiracy Theories about the events leading up to the invasion, including 9/11, especially seductive. What they might not realise is how Conspiracy Theories have been used to promote right-wing or anti-Semitic causes. By being outed as right-wing propaganda, Conspiracy Theories might be made less attractive to left-leaning individuals. The message to get across to such individuals is that being a Conspiracy Theorist means effectively allying oneself with people whose political outlook and objectives one usually finds repugnant. The actual history of Conspiracy Theories needs to be told and retold.

This approach won't work with right-leaning Conspiracy Theorists. They presumably won't be put out by the observation that many Conspiracy Theories have been used to promote right-wing causes. Some on the right might be embarrassed by the implicit or explicit anti-Semitism of popular Conspiracy Theories; but, if they aren't embarrassed, or if they insist that their theories are not anti-Semitic, then there is little hope of changing their minds by talking about the history of Conspiracy Theories. Where Conspiracy Theories are part and parcel of a broader political ideology, the only way to respond to them is to criticise the ideology. Conspiracy Theories do not exist in isolation. They are part of a larger theory about how the world works and can't be effectively undermined without tackling this larger theory.

Stage two of an effective political response to Conspiracy Theories is more straightforward. A factor in the thinking of many conspiracy apologists, if not Conspiracy Theorists themselves, is the concern that people who attack Conspiracy Theories are, if not actual government agents, still doing the government's dirty work. After all, it's undeniable that Conspiracy Theories tend to identify the government or its agents as conspirators. It's also undeniable that there is plenty of evidence of government misconduct in liberal democracies as well as in totalitarian states. One can argue about how often that misconduct takes the form of conspiracies, but there can be no debate about the frequency with which governments of all political persuasions in all political systems behave badly and expect to get away with it.

That being so, doesn't it follow that being a critic of Conspiracy Theories means being an apologist for the poor behaviour of people in power that Conspiracy Theories are trying to highlight?

From this standpoint it doesn't particularly matter whether a particular Conspiracy Theory is literally true. What matters is the bigger picture, the fact that governments and their agents are often up to no good. The general point stands regardless of the merits of a given Conspiracy Theory, and people who attack Conspiracy Theories are denying a deeper truth about politics and power to which these theories give expression.

One might call this the 'Oliver Stone' defence, in honour of the director of the movie *JFK*. After its release in 1991 the movie was lambasted by critics for being riddled with inaccuracies and for promoting a Conspiracy Theory about the Kennedy assassination that owed much more to the fertile imagination of Jim Garrison than to the known facts. In response to the charge that his movie was a piece of shameless propaganda, Stone responded with the priceless assertion that, while he didn't claim that it told a true story, his movie did speak an 'inner truth' or, in the words of *JFK*'s star Kevin Costner, an 'emotional truth'.[8]

Tempting as this line of thinking might be, it should be resisted. 'Inner truths' are no substitute

---

[8] J. Leo, 'Oliver Stone's paranoid propaganda', at https://www.pbs.org/wgbh/frontline/article/oliver-stones-paranoid-propaganda.

for the actual truth, and you don't need to be a Conspiracy Theorist to be a critic of government misconduct. In reality, being a Conspiracy Theorist makes it harder to be an effective critic. This point came up in the last chapter in relation to Noam Chomsky's criticisms of the foreign policy of successive American governments. If you are against US policy in the Middle East, then be against it; don't confuse matters by dressing up your criticisms in the garb of a Conspiracy Theory. The problem with the idea that the literal truth of a Conspiracy Theory is less important than the bigger picture is that it plays right into the hands of the very people whom Conspiracy Theorists want to criticise.

How so? Because it's easier for governments to dismiss criticism of their conduct if they can point to factual inaccuracies in these criticisms. A good rule of thumb for government critics should be not to do anything to diminish their own credibility, and this means not flirting with speculative and esoteric Conspiracy Theories for which there is no real evidence. Not worrying about the literal truth of one's accusations and focusing on the bigger picture is self-defeating because it's easier for other people to ignore the bigger picture when they can point to obvious flaws in one's theories. It's always best to stick with the known facts and avoid ill-informed speculation.

It's just not true, therefore, that critics of Conspiracy Theories are doing the government's dirty work. Governments might have an interest in subverting Conspiracy Theories, but they aren't helped by critics of Conspiracy Theories who are as forthright in their criticisms of government policies. When it comes to the important questions about government social, foreign and economic policy, Conspiracy Theories are a red herring. The effect of knocking them out is to clear the ground for a serious discussion of the real issues, including the many ways in which governments *actually* screw up. Why focus on imaginary wrongs when there are real wrongs to put right?

This leads me to the next point: an effective political strategy against Conspiracy Theories needs to stress the distinction between Conspiracy Theories and conspiracy theories. Failure to do so leaves one open to accusations of bad faith or naïvety. Conspiracy Theorists like to defend their theories by pointing to well-documented examples of actual conspiracies such as Watergate or Operation Northwoods. In reply, one needs to acknowledge that theories about conspiracies can be well founded. However, to state the obvious, just because some theories about conspiracies are well founded, it doesn't follow that they all are. The plausibility of one conspiracy theory doesn't extend to all others. On the other hand, accepting that some conspiracy theories have turned out to be true should help to correct any impression that one can see no wrong when it comes to government conduct.

The simplest and most effective way to make these points is to use the distinction I drew in chapter 1 between conspiracy theories and Conspiracy Theories. A conspiracy theory is a well-founded theory about a conspiracy, a theory that has the backing of documentary and other relevant evidence. Many conspiracy theories, such as the one about the Gunpowder Plot, are uncontroversially true, though it's conceivable that even a well-established conspiracy theory might turn out to be mistaken. Conspiracy theories might serve a political purpose, but that isn't their *raison d'être*. In contrast, Conspiracy Theories are *essentially* political and, given all their other distinctive features, are unlikely to be true. A Conspiracy Theory isn't a theory like any other theory and shouldn't be treated as such.

By drawing this distinction and allowing that there are well-founded conspiracy theories about government misconduct, Conspiracy Theory critics can dismiss any suggestion of bad faith or naïvety. The response to the suggestion that governments and other powerful groups of people sometimes conspire should be: 'Of course they do!' There was never any question of denying that. The objection is to speculative, esoteric, amateurish, self-sealing, premodern and contrarian theories about conspiracies.

A response to this might be to argue that one person's Conspiracy Theory is another person's conspiracy theory. It's all very well distinguishing between justified conspiracy theories and unjustified Conspiracy Theories, but who is to say which is which? Isn't it all relative? For a 9/11 Conspiracy Theorist, his theory is a justified conspiracy theory, whereas the official account is an unjustified Conspiracy Theory. From the official point of view the opposite is the case. Who decides who is right and who is wrong?

The facts decide. Since there are always going to be arguments about what the actual facts are and what they show, there are always going to be arguments about whether a particular theory is a conspiracy theory or a Conspiracy Theory. But that doesn't mean that there is no fact of the matter or that the truth is relative. When someone claims that aircraft impacts couldn't have brought down the twin towers, that person is making a testable claim that is either true or false. As with all such claims, all we have to go on is experience and the opinion of people with the relevant expertise. If most experts believe that a claim is false, then that is a legitimate reason for classifying any theory based on it as a Conspiracy Theory rather than as a conspiracy theory. People may have differing opinions about what the facts are, but actual facts are never a matter of opinion.

It would be easier to make these points if Conspiracy Theorists were the only people who tout Conspiracy Theories. As Kathryn Olmsted notes, many Americans have developed Conspiracy Theories in response to the official Conspiracy Theories proposed by the government.[9] She gives many examples of officially sanctioned Conspiracy Theories, including the theory that Iraq was in some way involved in 9/11. It's hard to object to other people's Conspiracy Theories if you yourself are a Conspiracy Theorist. If you want to resist the spread of Conspiracy Theories, then don't spread Conspiracy Theories. An obvious point, but one

---

[9] Kathryn Olmsted, *Real Enemies: Conspiracy Theories and American Democracy, World War I to 9/11* (Oxford University Press, 2009).

that needs to be made in the light of what Olmsted says.

The fact that governments themselves are responsible for so many Conspiracy Theories is one more reason for insisting that being anti-Conspiracy Theory is not the same thing as being pro-government or pro-establishment. In the United States today, Donald Trump and the Republican Party are the establishment and both have promoted Conspiracy Theories, for example the theory that protestors against the appointment of Brett Kavanaugh to the US Supreme Court were part of a conspiracy orchestrated by George Soros. As *New York Times* columnist Paul Krugman notes, when people who hold most of the levers of power promote Conspiracy Theories, their aim is to delegitimise opposition and to create excuses for punishing anyone who dares to criticise their actions.[10] How, in that case, can it possibly be true that being opposed to Conspiracy Theories makes one some kind of government lackey?

These political responses to Conspiracy Theories are all worth pursuing, but their effectiveness is bound to be limited. Not even moderate Conspiracy

---

[10] P. Krugman, 'The paranoid style in G.O.P. politics', *New York Times*, 8 October 2018.

How to Respond to Conspiracy Theories

Theorists will necessarily be convinced, let alone hard-core ones. It's not that Conspiracy Theories are impossible to rebut. Rebutting them can be hard work but, as Posner demonstrates, it is possible. Why do such rebuttals carry so little weight with many Conspiracy Theorists? Why is it so hard to stop the spread of Conspiracy Theories and convince people to give up theirs?

This is partly because, as I've stressed, such theories are nothing if not seductive in all the ways that I described in chapter 2. Or perhaps it would be more accurate to say that they are seductive to people with a certain mindset, one that looks for a hidden meaning in mundane events. Related to this is the sheer passion and determination of the conspiracy lobby. For many Conspiracy Theorists, their theories are an obsession and an expression of who they are. Not unreasonably, they construe attacks on their theories as personal; and they don't take such attacks lying down. Few of their critics can match the stamina of Conspiracy Theorists, their willingness to keep going. It's hard to outlast a Conspiracy Theorist – or to be as angry.

To make things even more difficult, there is the role of the Internet. It's often suggested that the Internet promotes the spread of Conspiracy Theories and makes it harder to do anything about it. The

116

Internet increases the accessibility of Conspiracy Theories and the speed with which they can be transmitted from one person to another. In the days before the Internet it took weeks or months for a Conspiracy Theory to gain traction with significant numbers of people. Now all it takes is a click or tap to pass on a Conspiracy Theory. Another factor is the existence of online communities of Conspiracy Theorists who reinforce one another's theories and add to the general hysteria after major political events. In effect, Conspiracy Theorists radicalise one another, that is, egg one another on to embrace ever more extreme theories without any risk of pushback.

But if the Internet is part of the problem, then it is also part of the solution. True, the Internet makes Conspiracy Theories more accessible; but it also makes it easier to rebut them. Imagine a person whose curiosity about Holocaust-denying Conspiracy Theories leads him to the idea that Hitler didn't order the extermination of the Jews in Europe. It's easy enough to locate more information about this online, much easier than it would have been before the days of the Internet. But a quick Google search of David Irving reveals that he was found by a court to have deliberately distorted the historical evidence in order to promote Holocaust denial.

Why did the court come to this conclusion? Because of the testimony of experts, including Evans. This might, then, lead one to Evans's testimony and to his rebuttal of Irving's 'evidence'. One is now in a position to understand not just *that* Irving is wrong but, more importantly, *why* he is wrong. If challenged by a Conspiracy Theorist to explain what is wrong with Irving's view, one is now in a position to do so. It is the Internet that one has to thank for that, even if it is also true that one would never have heard of Irving in the first place without the Internet.

The same goes for other Conspiracy Theories. The truth is out there; one only has to look. For virtually every unfounded Conspiracy Theory, there are easily accessible detailed explanations of their defects. Hard-core Conspiracy Theorists won't be interested in these explanations and won't accept them even if they encounter them. But there is still hope for the uncommitted or curious. The Internet spreads the poison of Conspiracy Theories but also the antidote.

Beyond making the point that the Internet can be used to undermine Conspiracy Theories as well as to spread them, what can be done in *practical* terms to deter the uncommitted or curious from becoming fully paid-up Conspiracy Theorists? The Internet is a vast store of information, misinformation and disinformation. Disinformation is simply misinformation that is dressed up to look like information. Its purpose is to mislead or deceive, and there are many Conspiracy Theories whose aim is to do precisely that. For example, the claim that Sandy Hook was a false flag isn't just misinformation. It is disinformation. How can we tell the difference?

One suggestion is that the key to this, and to preventing the spread of Conspiracy Theories, is education. If it's as hard as I've been suggesting to change the minds of committed Conspiracy Theorists, then it makes more sense to focus on preventing people from becoming Conspiracy Theorists in the first place. Among other things, this means educating children from a young age to spot the difference between information and disinformation. This is how the journalist Matthew d'Ancona puts it:

Information overload means that we must all become editors: sifting, checking, assessing what we read. Just as children are taught how to understand printed texts their critical faculties should be trained to meet the very different challenges of a digital feed ... It should be a core task of primary – not secondary

– education to teach children how to select and discriminate from the digital torrent. Learning how to navigate the web with discernment is the most pressing cultural mission of our age.[11]

This educational response to the spread of Conspiracy Theories clearly has a lot going for it. It connects with philosophical ideas about so-called *intellectual virtues* like open-mindedness, critical thinking, respect for evidence and curiosity. Intellectual virtues are personal qualities that help us in our pursuit of knowledge and understanding. The hope is that by developing such virtues at an early age people can be immunised against Conspiracy Theories by learning to see for themselves what is wrong with them. A particularly helpful feature of d'Ancona's way of putting things is its emphasis on *discernment*. Being able to tell the difference between trustworthy and untrustworthy sources is ultimately a matter of *judgement*, of having a feel for this sort of difference.

And yet there are reasons for thinking that, despite its obvious appeal, the educational response to the spread of Conspiracy Theories has its limitations

---

[11] M. d'Ancona, *Post-Truth: The New War on Truth and How to Fight Back* (Ebury Press, 2017), pp. 113–14.

and needs to be supplemented by other approaches. One limitation, of course, is that it's too late for many people. Those who have missed out on the kind of education that d'Ancona describes will remain as vulnerable as ever to the tactics of Conspiracy Theorists.

Another consideration is that the intellectual virtues that I have described as protecting people from falling for Conspiracy Theories might be seen as the very virtues that, in an exaggerated form, are part of the conspiracist mindset. It isn't true, after all, that the Conspiracy Theorist is not open-minded or curious. What could be more open-minded than being willing to consider the possibility that the moon landings were faked? It's no accident, therefore, that Conspiracy Theorists see themselves as intellectually virtuous and their establishment critics as displaying intellectual vices like closed-mindedness and lack of curiosity.

Perhaps, in that case, the real criticism of Conspiracy Theorists is not that they aren't open-minded but that they are *too* open-minded. Being too open-minded can make a person gullible, gullible enough to take seriously even the most bizarre Conspiracy Theories. However, it is a delicate matter to say what counts as being too open-minded or not open-minded enough. It is easy to accuse other people of lacking intellectual virtue, but the predictable retort is to accuse the accuser of exactly the same intellectual failings. This retort may or may not be correct, but it does suggest that attacking Conspiracy Theorists on purely intellectual grounds is unlikely to be effective.

Apart from the issue of effectiveness, it's also not right to put so much emphasis on intellectual factors. After all, while Conspiracy Theorists who deny the Holocaust might have intellectual failings, their moral failings are surely far more significant. The main thing they lack is moral rather than intellectual virtue. Perhaps, in the end, moral and intellectual virtue can't be sharply separated. Nevertheless, it is easier to make the case that people who promote racist Conspiracy Theories are morally objectionable than to show that they are intellectually deficient. Even if they are intellectually deficient, that's not really the point.

This raises a deeper question about the nature of argument and conviction. All this talk of the intellectual virtues needed to stop people from becoming Conspiracy Theorists in the first place assumes that belief in Conspiracy Theories is fundamentally an intellectual matter. In much the same way, my discussion of the prospects of changing the minds of people who are already Conspiracy

Theorists assumed that minds are changed, if at all, by intellectual considerations or rational argument. However, as the philosopher David Hume pointed out in the eighteenth century, belief is, at least partly, a matter of feeling. Reason, Hume famously argued, is the slave of the passions. If this is correct, then the best way to influence what people believe is to appeal to their feelings and emotions, not just their intellects.

Which emotions? This is where what I have described as the 'outing' of Conspiracy Theories as anti-Semitic or as right-wing propaganda becomes important. The point of trying to show that many Conspiracy Theories are anti-Semitic or peddling right-wing propaganda is to shame or embarrass people into not flirting with them. Shame and embarrassment are *emotions*. If a proto-Conspiracy Theorist is embarrassed to discover that Conspiracy Theories have historical links with anti-Semitism, her embarrassment is an expression of her *values*. The truth is that values count for more than abstract reasoning in political debate. If anti-Semitism is the original sin of Conspiracy Theories, that is something that good people will care about. Not caring about it is a sign that one is *morally* deficient.

What is starting to emerge, then, is a multitrack strategy for dealing with Conspiracy Theories and the people who promote them. The three components of this strategy are:

- Rebuttal: wherever possible, use arguments and evidence to rebut Conspiracy Theories.
- Education: equip people at an early age with the critical thinking skills and intellectual virtues that will help them to distinguish between truth and lies, information and disinformation. But education must also include moral education about the evils of the racist and extremist ideologies that it is the function of Conspiracy Theories to promote.
- Outing: make sure that people have a proper understanding of the function of Conspiracy Theories as propaganda and of the causes they promote.

None of these strategies is likely to be successful on its own. But, taken together, they might be more effective.

The battle against Conspiracy Theories is neverending. As one Conspiracy Theory is rebutted or fades away, others will take its place. Fifty years from now there will still be Conspiracy Theories and Conspiracy Theorists. They won't be obsessing about 9/11 or the assassination of JFK. Instead, they will have new theories about events that have not yet happened. But this is no excuse for giving up. We need to be as relentless in opposing Conspiracy Theories as the Conspiracy Theorists are in spreading them. If this book has a single take-home message, it is this: Conspiracy Theories are harmful. To understand this, and to understand all the different ways in which they are harmful, is to understand that not fighting back against them is simply not an option.

Further Reading

Cassam, Q. *Vices of the Mind: From the Intellectual to the Political* (Oxford University Press, 2019).

Coady, D. (ed.). *Conspiracy Theories: The Philosophical Debate* (Ashgate, 2006).

Uscinski, J. (ed.). *Conspiracy Theories and the People Who Believe Them* (Oxford University Press, 2019).

Uscinski, J. and J. Parent. *American Conspiracy Theories* (Oxford University Press, 2014).